Newspaper Clippings courtesy of Salmon Arm Observer, Shoppers
Guide and Eagle Valley News

Acknowledgements

Front cover: Thank you to my Daughter **Tina Goodale** for
designing and hand painting the cover for the book.

Editing: Thank you to my Daughter **Sarah Goodale** for editing
the book and keeping it as close to the original diary as possible.

Special thank you to my wife **Vi** for her continued support
throughout the years in encouraging me to complete the book.

Thank you to **Darryl** and **Max** for helping make this adventure
possible and believing in the "buddy system"

27 Days Around Shuswap Lake
A True Story

27 Days Around Shuswap Lake is a true story that took place in the province of British Columbia in 1979.

Shuswap Lake is a beautiful lake, nestled in the heart of British Columbia. It is known as the Houseboat Capital of Canada. The lake caters to hundreds of thousands of tourists each and every year. For generations, people thought the shoreline around Shuswap Lake was 1,000 miles or more.

A local newspaper (The Shoppers Guide) offered a challenge for someone to measure the distance of the shoreline by circumnavigating it on foot. It was this challenge that was offered and accepted; that would change my life.

The story is written from my personal diary that I kept during our 27 days around this beautiful lake. This book is a warm story for people of all ages. It tells of our hardships, emotions and determination of attempting to complete a task that had never before been attempted.

This story shares the true Canadian experience of the outdoors with its readers, and tells of the appreciation for Mother Nature, and the respect for God's country.

ABOUT SHUSWAP LAKE

Shuswap Lake is located in the interior of British Columbia and is midway between Calgary and Vancouver. The name Shuswap is named after the Shuswap Indians, northernmost of the Great Salishan Family, one of the largest tribes in the interior of British Columbia. This tribe once numbered more than 5,000 people, who were fishermen and hunters who roamed in bands over the vast area of lakes and forests.

Shuswap Lake is made up of four large arms. These arms are called Shuswap Lake Main Arm, Salmon Arm, Anstey Arm, and Seymour Arm. All of these arms converge at Cinemousun Narrows. The lake is surrounded by some of the most beautiful scenes that one could imagine. The area around Shuswap Lake is surrounded by outstanding natural beauty.

The glowing moonlight, as it reflects on the lake; reveals the shadows of trees and mountains and is unbelievable. The stars are so big and bright; you feel like you can reach up and touch them. The lake is like a magnet that draws you to it. You can't seem to take your eyes off of it.

The MV Phoebe Ann is a regular sight on Shuswap Lake. The Phoebe Ann is a barge that can carry approximately 40 passengers, and a few canoes up and down various parts of the lake, stopping at several locations. Nestled on the south shores of Shuswap Lake is a town called Salmon Arm, also known as The Northern Gateway to the Okanagan.

Salmon Arm first started as a railway camp during the construction of the Canadian Pacific Railway and got its name from the large runs of Salmon that used to run up the creeks that empty into Shuswap Lake.

Shuswap Lake has some very rugged shoreline. A large portion of the shoreline, especially in the Anstey Arm area is rocky. There are several cliffs, some stemming quite high above the ground. There is also low lying bush, flush with the edge of the water. In some areas there are beaches.

It is very mossy in the forest areas of the North side of the lake, due to lack of sunlight and dampness. There are also many trails, where people cross country ski in the winter. The Shuswap Lake area has plenty of sudden and frequent storms that can show up at any moment. The water level rises and falls every year. Mid-June and July are the peaks, depending on the winter's snowfall. The highest the water level has ever been was back in 1972. Previous to that, the highest level was in 1949.

Shuswap Lake is a fresh water lake. The water is very cold most of the year except in the areas where there are beaches. Rainbow trout and lake trout are the most common fish caught, although catching a ling cod is acceptable.

There are many creeks and a few rivers flowing into Shuswap Lake, all with water that is crystal clear. Shuswap Lake seems to be hidden in the midst of the surrounding mountains. The water flows where ever it wants to, as it winds and twists past many corners. The winds on the lake are strong, and the breeze is mild.

This area is a suitable area for any kind of wildlife; eagle, hawk, crow, pheasant, are only a few of the many species of birds that can be found around the lake. Not to mention that 'ole hummingbird'.

Some of the larger wildlife that can be found are cougar, lynx, bear, deer and moose. Beaver, otter and porcupine also enjoy the environment. There are plenty of snakes too and let's not forget Mr. Chipmunk. There are logging camps around the lake and Shuswap Lake is known as the Houseboat Capital of Canada. There are lighthouses at each major point, to guide boats the night. Shuswap Lake is the home for retired people, vacationers and people just wanting to get away from it all on weekends.

No one around the lake is without a boat. Whether it is a canoe, or cabin cruiser, everyone is well equipped. The Shuswap is a part of nature that should never be tampered with. The way it is laid out is just amazing. It has every scene that a person would want, and even more. It has both wilderness and civilization. To sum it all up, everything that you can dream of is found here.

"Mother Nature owns this land, and it is she, who keeps it beautiful, in every way."

PREFACE

The following book that you are about to read is all fact and non-fiction. It covers the time between May 19, 1979 and June 15, 1979.

It tells of our feelings, our emotions and our fight to defeat the hardships and obstacles, in our 27 day incredible journey around Shuswap Lake.

Yes, this would be the test for any man, challenging the wilds. Without further a due, please read on about the adventures of the lake walkers.

INTRODUCTION

The story begins when I traveled to Salmon Arm, British Columbia during the summer of 1978 to visit my Brother Larry, who I hadn't seen for some time.

While staying in Salmon Arm, I would pick up the two local newspapers to read. The Salmon Arm Observer and The Shoppers Guide. These two newspapers would be available each week, and I looked forward to reading them.

One day while browsing through the Shoppers Guide, a small magazine inserted into the newspaper fell out called The Visitors Guide. This suited me just fine, because that's just what I was, a visitor.

As I was flipping through the pages, my attention was attracted to the bottom of page thirty six. At the bottom of page thirty-six, there was a small article suggesting that someone should walk the entire shoreline of Shuswap Lake wearing a pedometer, to settle the long-disputed controversy over the shoreline miles.

Estimates in the past had varied between 300 and 1,000 miles and more. This was enough for me, as the article stayed in the back of my head for quite some time. I had picked up a summer job and spent most of the summer studying Shuswap Lake, and asking some people that I met if they were interested in taking on the task.

I couldn't find anyone local who wanted to go on this trip. I think they may have even thought I was crazy to think of such an idea, let alone, how long it would take. I am also a firm believer in the buddy system, and braving the wilds by myself was just too risky.

I travelled back to Ontario, bringing with me the idea of possibly being the first person to take on such an undertaking. I arrived back in Stoney Creek, Ontario, and while visiting my friends,; telling them about my trip out west, I suggested that someone should come with me on this journey. A few were interested but again it was like a joke to most of them. I don't even think my friends thought that I would attempt this walk.

One night close to Christmas, I asked a long-time friend of mine, Darryl Kelly, if he would be interested in coming along with me. Darryl had to finish school, but thought a trip of this nature would be good for him at this point in his life.

It was decided Christmas Eve that our goal in 1979 would be to walk the entire shoreline of Shuswap Lake. We had saved up our money and shortly after Christmas both Darryl and I finished school and we moved to Calgary, Alberta. We found work at Russell Steel in Calgary. Our plans were to work until summer, and try to get some time off to walk the entire shoreline of Shuswap Lake.

April 15 came, and we started making plans for the trek. It was a rainy afternoon when we drove to Salmon Arm to see if anyone had attempted the walk. Keep in mind that almost one year has passed from the time I had read the article, but amazingly enough, no one had even looked into it. Our chance was still there.

We checked with the Mayor (Mayor Margaret Lund), The Salmon Arm Observer, and the Shoppers Guide to try to track down the article that was published. I couldn't remember where I had read it. One year can be a long time.

Finally, Jim Scales who had his office right next door to the Shoppers Guide; suggested that it may be in the Visitors Guide. The employees of The Shoppers Guide were nice enough to let us search through back issues of their weekly newspaper, and it was their help, along with Jim's, that led us to what we were looking for.

There it was, right in front of us, boy, was I relieved. I always thought that Darryl might not have believed me, but there it was. Now we had to inquire about more information. Sally Scales, the owner of The Shoppers Guide, was not in and we needed to talk with her to find out exactly how to go about this. We drove back to Calgary so excited and happy that no one else had even inquired.

The next day we went to work and asked our boss if we could have the time off to attempt this walk. At first, he said it was not a problem. We told him that we would need from July 1st until possibly mid-August, in order to complete this trek.

Darryl and I started to think that it may be to our benefit to move to Salmon Arm and start studying the Lake much closer. We had already read quite a bit about the lake, and studied topographical maps, but we needed as much information as we could get.

During our day trips to Salmon Arm, we met an older man who lived in Salmon Arm- who was interested in what we were about to do. His name was Tony Wawrzniak. Tony was 80 years of age, and was a great outdoors man from Poland.   Tony knew the area well, and suggested that we start the journey much earlier to "compensate for high water".

This made sense to us, because if we waited until July 1st, the streams around the lake would thaw from the warmer temperatures, and flow into Shuswap Lake, raising the water level. We would have had less shoreline to walk on. It was just after we talked about the risk of high water that we decided to start this trek May 19th, rather than the July 1st plan.

Our commitment to this task was getting stronger every day, and we went back to our boss in Calgary to discuss having the leave of absence earlier. This time the answer was no. Although the company understood what we wanted to do and were supportive of us, they just couldn't give us the changed time off.

We had saved quite a bit from working in Calgary, and decided that we couldn't keep commuting from Alberta to British Columbia, so we decided to move to Salmon Arm. After setting up in Salmon Arm, (an apartment above Adam and Eve Hairstyling on Hudson Street), we wasted no time in starting to train.

Darrell Kelly, left, and Dan Goodale moved to Salmon Arm from Calgary last week because of an item in last year's Visitors' Guide. They have come to measure the shoreline around Shuswap Lake, and they will do it on foot.

Dan lived in Salmon Arm last summer and read the item in the Visitors' Guide which said estimates of the lake's shoreline vary from 400 to 1,000 miles, with the suggestion that someone should walk the shore, wearing a pedometer, which we would provide.

The two men plan to train for the next two months, and they will look for sponsors for their estimated month-long trek. They will be studying maps, and will familiarize themselves with the area.

Because they do not know Shuswap Lake, they have a request: would someone take them on a boat tour of the lake, or part of it? Call the Shoppers' Guide.

We have a question. What is a pedometer?

Sally Scales photo

Shortly after moving to Salmon Arm, Darryl's step brother Max Wilde came out for a visit. Max knew nothing about the walk, and when we explained to him what we were going to try to do, Max was very interested in transporting our supplies by canoe. This sounded really good to us, and would allow us to take more supplies then we had originally planned.

This would be quite the challenge for Max. He would be the first person ever to canoe the entire shoreline of Shuswap Lake, which is a huge task in itself. Max had done plenty of canoeing, especially in Algonquin Park in Northern Ontario, and several other rivers, but nothing like Shuswap Lake. .

Our next job was to try to get local sponsors to gather interest in what we were talking about doing, and sponsor us with anything that would help us out on this estimated trek of four to six weeks.

We canvassed store after store, introduced ourselves, and spoke with all of the owners about our plans to walk around the lake. They were all very interested in what we were going to do, and sponsor us with everything we needed to get started on our fierce journey.

We received everything from mosquito oil, bandages, food, and camera equipment (to document a slide essay for the town). It was unbelievable; the support that the town showed us.

An information booth was set up at Cedarvale Center in order for the public to come and meet us and ask questions. A tent, hiking boots, sleeping bags, and many more items were offered. A second hand store (Mainline Prize) even lent us a Coleman stove to use. The Salmon Arm Parks and   Leisure Department offered a canoe for Max to use.

Getting all set to go!

Darrel Kelly, left, and Dan Goodale are getting set to walk around Shuswap Lake, but they aren't going to wait until July 1st. They have decided to leave about May 19th.

Tony Wawrzyniak of Salmon Arm has been giving them a lot of good advice, and it was he who suggested they leave sooner, before the water level in Shuswap Lake is too high.

Tony also suggested they should take along a canoe for carrying their gear and food, and they plan on doing just that. A third member of their party is Max Wilde, Darrel's half-brother, and he will be the canoeist.

The Shuswap will get a lot of publicity from this adventure, and the two men who plan to walk around the lake will get a lot of exposure. So far, they have an appointment to appear on television, and they will be interviewed for radio. A large party is being planned when they leave the wharf, and an even larger one is planned for their return.

Before they can begin their journey, the men need supplies. They need a canoe, a three-man tent, hiking boots (one size 9 and one size 10), a 22 rifle and ammunition, a first-aid kit, hunting knives, a little stove with fuel, and food. Money would be appreciated, too, in the form of pledges.

They plan to be in a booth in Cedarvale Centre during the next two Saturdays. You will be able to meet them, and discuss their trip with them. They will gladly take donations from you for their journey.

Two television interviews were arranged. One interview was on BCTV with host Mike Roberts in Kelowna, and the second interview was on CHBC TV with host Russ Richardson. The program was called 'Let's Visit'. What an experience it was, driving to Kelowna to be interviewed on television about a challenge that nobody has ever attempted. We were very nervous but managed to get through it. It was so funny watching ourselves on television from our apartment. We felt like we were celebrities!

Even stamp collectors were getting excited. We had envelopes made up with an outline of Shuswap Lake printed in the top left corner with the date and position of our location. They were printed with '**First Walk Around Shuswap'** just above the lake, and we had determined nine checkpoints around the lake. We would mail these envelopes from each of the nine checkpoints as we progressed around the lake, and the stamp collectors would collect all nine envelopes with the locations on them. They would have these complete sets as a valued part of their collection.

The interest was building quite rapidly now and there was no way of backing out. In fact, we knew that no matter what we would have to complete this trek, even if we had a broken leg. The determination got stronger with everyone's interest. We were getting prepared mentally, but it was now time to exercise our bodies to the punishment that our bodies would be taking during this adventure. We had done some earlier exercises, but as we got out on the lake to see some of the shoreline, we knew that we better work on ourselves far more than we had. This walk would be harder than we had imagined. Now it was time to really realize what we were up against.

OKANAGAN VALLEY TELEVISION COMPANY LIMITED
TELEX: 048-5119   PHONE (604) 762-4535

342 LEON AVENUE, KELOWNA, B.C.
CANADA V1Y 6J2

Dan Goodale,

To find how far it is around something is as good a reason to go for a walk as any.

Take care on your journey and don't let Shuswap Lake's shores be you last.

Here's to old socks.

Mike Robert

SALLY SCALES LTD., BOX 1008, SALMON ARM, B.C. V0E 2T0 832-731:

CHBC
OKANAGAN TELEVISION

May 11/79

MEMO TO: Dan Goodale

FROM: **RUSS RICHARDSON**

Thanks for being an excellent guest on today's "Let's Visit" show & good luck with your Shuswap Walk.

Russ

342 LEON AVENUE, KELOWNA, B.C.   V1Y 6J2 — 762-4535

**First Walk Around
Shuswap Lake**

Salmon Arm   Sicamous

Date	Position	

PREPARATION

In preparation for this incredible journey, we would walk from Canoe Point Road every day for more than two weeks. We jogged five miles a day, twice a day for three weeks. We hiked up Mount Ida, and did calisthenics on a regular basis. Weight lifting was done one hour a day, and our food intake was cut down. Beer was cut out, although we hated that part.

When we needed to go somewhere, we would walk instead of drive, and thin-soled shoes were worn to tighten up our feet. I would wear a pair of moccasins instead of my regular shoes as well.

We could feel our bodies getting stronger, as we would eat plenty of raw eggs daily for protein. Two vitamins and plenty of juices were also important to our health. We knew at times on this trek we would have to rely on our energy level to get over some of the obstacles that we had spotted when we were studying the lake at an earlier time. The preparation was very tough, as we did plenty of mountain climbing, and not to mention breaking in those hiking boots.

And so it was; that it was getting closer and closer to send off. All that was needed now was to put the means of recording the mileage to the test. We are using Taymor Pedometers, but before I continue, let me explain what a pedometer is. A pedometer is a device used to measure distance while walking. Webster dictionary describes a pedometer as "an instrument which measures the distance walked, by recording the number of steps".

The pedometer operates on a pendulum part inside of it, and with each stride the pendulum is activated and records the distance moved. On the side of the pedometer is an adjustment that you set to your stride. Ninety percent of people have a two-foot stride, so you set the stride adjustment to two feet, which is the neutral position for most people.

Darryl and I both had a stride of two feet. We used the pedometer with us when we would walk from Canoe Point Road. We would walk from the mileage signs just out of town, and both pedometers were dead-on accurate. In fact, over a twenty mile stretch- the pedometers were only out by a one tenth of one kilometer between Darryl and I.

Although some people tend to think that a pedometer is only good on a flat surface, this is not so. During our test of the pedometer, we used it uphill, downhill, through bush, walking in sand and gravel, and as amazing as it sounds- the pedometer was very accurate.

The pedometer should be placed as close to the center of your waistline as possible, and then offset it by two inches. If put in your pocket; it will also record.

Please keep in mind that it was up to us to decide whether or not we felt that the Taymor Pedometer would be accurate enough for the journey.

In the end, it is our belief that after what we had put the Taymor Pedometer through; we accept it as a qualified form of measurement for the task that we are undertaking.

← BELT CLIP

← HINGE

← MAIN SUPPORT

TAYLOR

PEDOMETER

STRIDE

INDICATOR

PEDOMETER

They're really serious, these Shuswap walkers

By Fiona Coulter

These three are very serious about their intentions to walk the shoreline of the Shuswap. They have come from Ontario to perform a task never before attempted, and are bent on achieving it.

On a Thursday afternoon in April, Dan Goodale and Darrel Kelly came to the Shoppers' Guide and asked us for information about something Dan had read last June. Something about walking the Shuswap.

We get unusual inquiries at the Shoppers' Guide sometimes.

Handing over stacks of back issues, Dan and Darrel started searching for something they weren't even positive was published in this paper. They had to read practically every item and became quite discouraged.

At long last, Jim Scales, who has an office next to our Shoppers' Guide basement suite, suggested looking in the Visitor's Guide.

Tongue in cheek, there it was. A small item inviting someone to walk around the lake with a pedometer strapped to their leg, to accurately measure the shore's distance.

Dan decided to accept the invitation. But braving the wilds of the west, by oneself, on foot, for weeks on end, wasn't that inviting. So he persuaded Darrel to come along, "In case I break a leg."

Originally planning to start walking on the first of July, the team was warned about high water making their trek more difficult. Now they will be leaving on May 19. Max Wilde (centre) has joined them, to paddle the canoe that will carry their supplies. He plans to do some fishing, too.

The Department of Leisure Services has arranged for the lending of a canoe, and will supply pedometers. Carol Hutchinson loaned them an Instamatic camera and supplied them with film, so the highlights of their trip will be documented.

Forms are being printed so anyone meeting the "trekkers" can sign and send them to the Salmon Arm Chamber of Commerce. By this, the validity of their accomplishment will be supported by numerous people, providing proof for the Guiness Book of World Records.

Those are the most important arrangements already made. The pedometer, a canoe, a camera, and a means of proof. Nevertheless, much is yet to be done before they depart.

This is going to be a survival test, so their supplies must be carefully planned, especially food. Without proper food, the trekkers will be weary and weak before long. How long will their feet hold out, if they don't have proper boots? Dan, who doesn't normally wear socks, should be concerned about this.

Not to mention a good tent. The black gnats on the Shuswap are fierce at dusk. Perhaps they should take along some Penny Royal Oil to combat the insects.

Some say they will make it. Some say they won't. Some say "have a good time,' and shake their heads.

"If someone offered to swim Lake Ontario the shore would be crowded with spectators and press-people," says Dan. "It would be headline news."

The adventures of the "Shuswap Walkers" should be headline news. Support the cause and show that Salmon Arm and all the lake people want everyone to know how big and beautiful our lake really is.

To help their trip, pledge sheets are being circulated. Any money over that used for the trip will be donated by the Chamber of Commerce to a charity. There should be a contest to guess the right mileage, too, of course. And a departure party and a homecoming.

If you have ideas, or information vital to this trip, would like to donate or lend something the team could use, or would just like to come to the parties, please call the Shoppers' Guide at 832-7260 or the Observer at 832-2131, or the Chamber of Commerce at 832-6247. Or visit Cedarvale Centre next week, where you can meet the Shuswap Walkers.

THE NIGHT BEFORE

It was now Friday, May 18th, and the tension was building. Physically and mentally we were ready. The feeling was like winning the lottery. We were practically in shock and couldn't sleep; just thinking about our big day tomorrow.

There was a loud knock on the door, and there he was once again, Tony Wawrzniak. Tony was like a coach and he was always there for us. Tony helped us study topographical maps, and gave us plenty of advice too. He came to wish us all the best before we set off in the morning.

Once Tony had left, there was another knock at the door. This time, it was some of our friends from Calgary who had come up to wish us well on our journey. They had driven 241 miles just to wish us well, so we had to stay up to entertain them. We talked all night about the trip, and the events leading up to send off, being on television, getting sponsors, training, and whether or not we thought we would succeed. We really didn't mind because we couldn't have slept if we wanted to, and besides, we really weren't sure how long this trek would take so we wouldn't be seeing our friends for a while.

It was a rough night before the start of our walk, as our friends left at 6:00 a.m. It was getting down to the last few hours before send off, and what once was probably a dream- was fast becoming reality.

DAY 1

They're Off!

The Lakewalkers trip has been made possible through generous donations from the Salmon Arm Community, and the Lakewalkers wish to extend their thanks to : the Jock Shop; Ready Rexall; Hudson Restaurarant; NDP Headquarters; Salmon Valley Sports; Sally Scales and her co-workers . ATT Audio ; Shuswap Realty; Bedford's Western Drugs; The Observer; ; Overwaitea; Mainline Co-op; Shuwap Pharmacy; Carol Hutchison ; Fayden Electric; Salmon Arm Bakery ; Mitchells Auto Supply ; Tony Wawrzyniak; Dooug Browning ; Dept. of Recreation ; Mitchell's Variety Store; Darroch's ; The Wheeler ; and Hartnett's .

Dan Goodale, spray paint in hand, takes a first few steps onto the who-knows-how-long trip around the Shuswap.

Dan and Darryl Kelly will be on foot , marking their progress in orange paint and Max Wilde will transport their supplies by canoe

They will also have " sighting forms " to give out to people they meet along the way, these can be sent in and will mark the exact position of their whereabouts according to the Shuswap topographical map.

Today was the big day. We were to set out from Salmon Arm Marina at 10:00 a.m. and follow in an easterly direction toward Canoe, B.C. We were so tired from the night before, but the excitement of this trek defeated the tiredness.

We headed down to the marina at 8:00 a.m. and loaded our supplies into the canoe. We were hustling to get everything ready before the send-off. Ten o'clock came and a handful of people arrived to see us off.

We thought more people would have shown up, but this was also a long weekend and most of the people had left Salmon Arm for a long weekend elsewhere. We were very nervous and waited as long as we could for anyone else to arrive, before deciding to take off. We officially left Salmon Arm Marina at 10:15 a.m. on May 19th.

It was already getting hotter out by the time we left the marina, and we were glad to get going. The community of 'Canoe' was our first checkpoint. On the route to Canoe, we were immediately faced with marsh for nearly 3 miles. We had only been gone for one hour and the mosquito's had started biting us and we had sweat beaming down our faces.

From our knees down, we were soaking wet. It was only 11:15 a.m. and already the thermometer was pushing eighty degrees. From the marshy areas, we were then faced with rocky shoreline, where every step had to be taken with caution. One slip, and one would surely have a twisted ankle. We could see Max out in the canoe, and he was struggling with strong head-waves which made the canoeing more difficult.

We passed out questionnaires like the one seen below, so that our progress would be reliably monitored from people seeing us at some point in our journey. These forms would be filled out by people witnessing our walk, and then they would be sent to the Salmon Arm Chamber of Commerce. There they would later be displayed on a blown up map of Shuswap Lake. The names and flags of all the people who sent in the verification slips would then be pinned to the areas around the lake where they had met us. We are also spray painting our route, so that people will know where we are.

_____ of _____
NAME   MAILING ADDRESS

Darryl Kelly and Dan Goodale walking the shorelines of Shuswap Lake, and Max Wilde steering a canoe,
on _____, at _____ at _____
         DATE   TIME   LOCATION

Please send to: Salmon Arm Chamber of Commerce
                        Box 999
                        SALMON ARM, B.C.
                        V0E 2T0

"All spray painting was done below the high water mark".

We were about two miles from the Canoe Sawmill when we met up with Tony. We chatted with Tony for a bit and continued on. Tony not only gave us good advice before starting this trek, but was also going to verify and prove our progress. We are also mailing envelopes at each checkpoint as another form of proving our progress. These envelopes will be mailed to Tony, who is a local stamp collector, and then Tony can relay to the town and local newspapers where we are.

When we arrived at Canoe Sawmill, it was closed. We needed to go through the saw mill to get around the shoreline, as there were hundreds of logs packed like cigarettes on the shoreline, as well as the water. A man named Gary who was doing a maintenance job; let us walk through the saw mill. We gave Gary a sighting form to complete, and asked if he would send it to the Chamber of Commerce on our behalf.

Just after walking through the saw mill, we decided to stop for lunch and man were we hungry and tired. Already sun burnt and soaking wet, we checked each pedometer and both were dead on accurate. It felt so good to sit down, that it was hard to get back up.

Carrying on our trek, we were just too exhausted from our company from Calgary the night before, so we decided to set up camp at Annis Bay, between Canoe and Sicamous. We probably could have made Sicamous, but we had no energy left. Camp was quick to set up, and supper was already being prepared. We sat around for a while talking about the day's events and how far we would go tomorrow.

We were happy but yet optimistic about what would lie ahead for us.

The first day was coming to a close, and we already had blisters and hundreds of mosquito bites.

The rest of the night found Darryl and Max hitting the sack fairly early, while I stayed up for a while to enter my diary.

We were camping by the train tracks, and train after train went by making it very difficult to go to sleep. It was like sleeping in shifts, as the trains seem to come and go every hour. These were CP Rail freight trains.

After a while, I decided to turn in for the night. As I lay awake, all I could think about was that no matter what, we had to complete this trip.

Some of the night's eerie noises kept me awake for a while, but myself; as well, was quick to fall asleep.

DAY2

We awoke this morning at seven o'clock, as our daily plan was to walk as many miles as possible, from eight in the morning until around six at night.

A hearty breakfast consisting of whole wheat porridge and toast were cooked over an open fire. This, along with juice and two vitamins would keep us going only until lunch. Our supplies were very important to us. We had to rely on them. The amount of energy that we had burnt off, just in the first day, was enough to tell us how important our supplies were.

We expect to be out on this journey for at least one month. If anything happened to cut down our supplies, then we would be in trouble for sure. Breakfast was eaten up quickly. You had to, if you wanted seconds. After tearing down camp, we set off at eight fifteen. The sleep that we managed to get the night before was good for us. We were hoping we didn't have to camp beside another railway track again.

We came across rocky shoreline again, as we stepped each step further into the wilderness. It was a cooler day, but we were still sweating quite a bit anyway. We were approaching Sicamous, with the shoreline still rocky. We had a couple of slips, but nothing serious.

When we arrived in Sicamous, we met Tony once more. Tony had gone to see Gordon Mackie, the owner of the Phoebe Anne, a barge that made several trips up and down different of Shuswap Lake. Tony had asked Gordon to keep an eye open for us on his daily trips on the lake. Gordon said "no problem".
We handed out more sighting forms, and then had lunch on the beach, again, over an open campfire. Tony had lunch with us and then left. The cooler weather soon became damp, and then it started to rain.

It started raining so hard that out-came the ponchos. Our feet were already blistered, and it was difficult getting use to the terrain, as it seemed to change all the time. The rock sure was slippery when it was wet. After a while, the rainstorm turned into drizzle. What an uncomfortable feeling it was, wearing these ponchos, plunging through the bush.

Without thinking, Max went ahead of us, where we had to cross Eagle River. It was understood that any river that was too big to cross, we could boat directly across it. To prove that we only boated across the mouth of the river, a sighting form was handed out before going across, and another handed out after crossing the river. After waiting nearly two hours for Max, hoping he would realize his mistake, and seeing that the sun was going down fast, we flagged down a boat and the gentlemen drove us across the mouth of the river. He also sent in a questionnaire to verify that indeed- that was all he did do, was only drive us to the other side.

Yet again, we were faced with marsh as we plunged through, mile after mile. The rain had let up on us by now, so we were carrying our ponchos. We had met more people camping, and handed out more forms for them to complete and send in. We thought we had lost Max for sure, but these campers told us that he wasn't too far ahead of us, which made us feel better.

Well, there he was, sitting on a big rock waiting for us. He looked tired from paddling, but you could see his body getting stronger.
We talked with Max for a few minutes, and then continued on to Hungry Cove to camp for our second night. To us, it was a long miserable day, with bush, rock, and marsh to cross.

It was getting late, and this was the only spot around where you could pitch a tent. It sure was quiet, as darkness crept into us. You could hardly hear anything, not even a sound. I marked on the map where we were, and entered my diary again. We all sat up for about two hours, before it got so dark that we felt safer in the tent.

Again, leery on whether there were bear or not, I slept with both ears open. I thought I was the only one dozing on and off, but Darryl and Max were half awake too. We ended up hearing a heck of a lot of noise during the night, and even though we are three men, we were scared to a certain extent. I could almost hear Darryl and Max' hearts pounding out loud, mine was equally loud.

If we did have a bear attack of any kind, what were we to do? All that we had were .22 rifles, and they were only to scare the bears off. We knew the rifles were quite harmless against a bear, unless you got a lucky shot, but that's all we had.

Our breathing was heavy, wondering what was outside. No one was around for miles. We were sitting ducks. We had built the fires up before going to bed, and our supplies were anchored out in the canoe above five feet in the water.

Sometimes, even the crackle from the fire in the middle of the night was even enough to wake you up. After a while, the noise went away and it was hard to get back to sleep.

I finally dozed off once it got lighter out and I knew that we were all safe.

DAY 3

Up again this morning at seven o'clock. We had the same breakfast as day two. We also found that setting up camp and tearing it down in the morning was beginning to be fun, at least so far it was.

At some point on this trip, we knew that there was a good chance that we would be confronted by a 'hermit' or 'bush person', and we were warned about him running after us with a shotgun. We had heard several stories in town, about a person that lived out in the wilderness, who didn't like people. Well exactly one mile on both pedometers from where we had camped last night- was his place.

We practically camped right at his door. We could tell that this was his place just by looking at it. As we were getting closer and closer to his home, we could see the shape of an elderly man standing ever so still, staring at us, and not even making a move. We quietly whispered to each other, "do you see what I see?" We both acknowledged what we saw, as an eerie feeling came over us.

We felt helpless and didn't know what to expect. We approached cautiously, while he continued to stare at us, not making any moves at all. He must have watched us walking toward him for about fifteen minutes, before he started to move towards us.

Our hearts were beating very fast. He didn't chase us, as we had heard he might do- but rather he came to greet us. We were somewhat relieved that there was no confrontation, but we were still very nervous. He invited us into his makeshift cabin, and I'll tell you, I was very impressed.

I told Darryl to try to get some pictures of his home while I spoke with him, only because we weren't sure if he would allow us to photograph him. As I was talking with him (it was more like an interview), I found out that his name was Stanley Foy. He had no middle name. He was born in Brewster Lake, Ontario on September 15, 1899. He was about five foot 10 inches tall, had a bald head, with a white beard. His eyes resembled those of a bunny rabbit, with the red pigment in them.

Stanley Foy was a white man, who claims he lost his memory due to some unknown drug. He claims to have a wife and daughter living somewhere back in Ontario. He also said he owns a farm with lots of horses. He says that he misses his wife and daughter, and wants to go back home.

As for his other side; Stanley Foy talked about the devil and the "spirit of black cloud". He even sang a song about the spirit of the black cloud to us twice. He had strange beliefs, and as expected, he does not allow anyone to take pictures of him, but we managed to sneak a few anyway without his knowledge.

His home was a cabin made out of plywood with three sheets of orange tarp covering the roof. The inside walls are completely covered with cardboard nailed to them. Everything inside his home is homemade. The dressers and stools are homemade, and of excellent quality, I might add.

There is a single homemade bed in the corner that has hospital blankets covering it, and he has an old Eaton's wood stove inside to heat his domain. It was very hot inside his cabin, about eighty-five degrees I would say.

Both Darryl and I were very quiet, and didn't know what to think. I think we were both in shock. As Stanley took us outside his cabin, Max had pulled the canoe to shore and now joined us. Stanley showed us the two steel pails, which he washes his clothes in, complete with homemade clubs to beat them with. He also showed us a storage hole two and a half feet in the ground where he keeps his vegetables. I reached down into the hole and pulled out a few carrots that had been down in the hole for some time. These carrots were as fresh as could be. The gardens that Stanley keeps are planted with just about everything. There are also stacks of wood piled up for his wood stove.

Stanley has a green canoe that he admires, and he took the time to give Max a little tip on canoeing. Our visit with Stanley was coming to an end as we had to make up for lost time. He wished us good luck and we were off again.

Walking through Stanley's backyard, all we could see were animal-skeletons of some sort, hanging from trees. We figured it was just to keep evil spirits away. Our bones chilled at the thought of it. We continued walking along the rocky shoreline, and had to climb a high cliff as the shoreline came to an end. The only way around this obstacle was to climb up and over. As we were climbing (and always looking behind us for any animals of any kind); the thought of meeting with a real life hermit- seemed to grow on us more and more.

At the top of this cliff, we found Indian markings. These markings appeared to have been created with some sort of root juice, as they were not washable.

Several of the writings were symbols of Indians, and diagrams of the sun. We didn't know what the signs meant, so we continued back down this cliff to the shoreline below.

Again, Darryl and I had rough crossings. Water to our knees, climbing rocky shoreline, you name it. We stopped at marble point for lunch after climbing that steep mountain with Indian writings on it. More sighting forms were handed out. After lunch, determined to get to the Narrows that night- we continued on, and met more people who offered us coffee and tea. This slowed down our progress. It was great chatting with all of the different people that we met, or maybe we were starting to miss that part of civilization, as meeting someone was becoming far and few between.

Plunging on and on, we finally made it about two miles from the Narrows. With breaking blisters, sore feet, and overly tired, we came to a spot between two large rocks. There was some small rocky beach between these two large rocks, so we decided that this is where we would set up camp.

It felt good getting out of those wet hiking boots. The skin on our feet were pure white and wrinkly because of all of the sweat and soakers that we had received throughout the day. Even with powder, our feet were still damp. Camp was now set up, and we were finally relaxing. Darryl was shaving, Max was taking a bath in the lake, and I was once again- marking our route on the map, and filling in my diary for the day.

As I was entering the day's log, I heard a boat off in the distance. It sounded like it was getting closer to us. It seemed to take forever to reach us, as the buzzing sound of the motor seemed to get louder, one decibel at a time. We all looked towards it, as it was headed right for us.

As the boat pulled up, I went to help pull it onto the shore and was greeted by a lady reporter from the Eagle Valley News. This lady had come all the way out of Sicamous to see us for an interview. Elections were just around the corner, and she wanted to know whom we would vote for Prime Minister.

She interviewed us quite intensively, and stayed with us for about an hour asking us about our trip so far. We couldn't believe that someone would boat all the way out from Sicamous to see us, let alone to do an interview. The reporter finally left our campsite, and we started supper. After a hearty supper, consisting this time of all vegetables, we started a bon fire and sang songs. The boys didn't like my singing very much, so we put on the tape recorder instead. It was fun singing and listening to music. It sure took our minds off of a lot of pressure ahead of us.

It was time again to hit the hay and try to get some shuteye. As darkness quickly fell upon us we were awakened again, almost all night by loud thumping noises. When we peered out the tent to see what the noises were- you would have to fix your eyes on something that you thought you seen, and hope it moved or didn't move. That's how dark it was.

I was always worried about the supplies. Our rifles were always in the tent at night with the safely on at all times. Fortunately, that's all that we heard were noises, loud scary noises. Tomorrow we are setting our goal to try and make it to the end of Anstey Arm.

From The Eagle's Perch

In a last minute spot survey the News interviewed the three Lake Walkers, who are attempting to walk the lakeshore of the Shuswap.

The question of the week was, Who do you think will be elected and why? The answers were varied and interesting.

DARRELL KELLY

I feel it is a right to vote, however it doesn't make any difference if I vote. It does not really matter, it won't effect my life or my lifestyle. I'll continue in my own way, despite a possible government change.

DAN GOODALE

Prime Minister Trudeau will be re elected, because he is the only man with the experience for the position. I am a Liberal supporter, and I will not change.

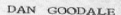

MAX WILDE

It is my first time to vote and I would like to see Joe Clark in as the Prime Minister of Canada. He deserves a chance.

DAY 4

Today we set our goal on reaching the tip of Anstey Arm, which is one of the four Arms that make up of Shuswap Lake. We were two hours from where we camped last night, when we spotted four black bears. We all carried whistles on us, and with Max canoeing- he could warn us of what was up ahead by blowing his whistle.

We heard his whistle go off and he started paddling toward shore to get a better look at what was there. He yelled out "bears!" Max then pulled into the shore and I took my rifle from the canoe and carried it for a while, just in case we accidentally came between a mother and her cub.

All we could hope for was to scare them off. They must have taken off, because the only trace left of them was body waste left on the rocks.

Again a speeding boat was heading toward us. This time it was no reporter. It was the R.C.M.P. from Sicamous. The Officer stopped us. I thought he was going to ask for the permit for my rifle, but he didn't. He told us "no more spray painting" because the phones were ringing off the walls at the police station in Sicamous, with complaints about the spray painting.

We said no problem and explained to the officer that all spray painting was done below the high water mark, and it would wash off when the water level in the lake rises. The officer asked us about our trek so far, and wished us well.

We are now hoping to see as many people as possible from here on in to verify our progress.

Lake walkers stir complaints

At last report the Shuswap Lake Walkers had rested up at Seymour Arm and were continuing on with their round-the-lake trek. However, their passage should be a little less visible from now on.

Dan Goodale and Darrel Kelly left Salmon Arm on the morning of May 19, planning to walk completely around Shuswap Lake. One of their objects is to determine the exact distance of the shoreline: a matter which has long been in dispute.

Accompanying them by canoe is Max Wilde who is transporting camping equipment and supplies.

The hikers were only a day or two out when complaints began to flood in to this paper, the radio station and police that the walkers were defacing the countryside by marking their passage on rock faces and other locations with large writings in fluorescent paint.

Some reports indicate painted messages several feet high and up to 40 feet in length; and that raised the wrath of many Shuswap residents.

Reports indicate police have now caught up with the trio and have put a stop to the paint marking.

The scenery here was just beautiful, and the terrain rough and rocky, with low lying bush covering most of the shoreline. So far it has been a fairly rough trip, and sometimes during the day all you do is stare at the ground as your walking to make sure of your balance.

If you could imagine walking on sharp rock, piled up, about a foot from the ground almost all day, it will give you a picture of how hard it was to keep good- footing, especially with wet hiking boots.

So far the only people we have met on Anstey Arm have a floating cabin at Pete Martin Creek. They were very nice to us, and warned us of the terrain up ahead of us. We started to laugh, saying "sure, it can't be as bad as what we had already been through. Can it?"

Well, we were wrong for the next eight miles, wow, was it rough-going. There were devils' club, which is a small thorny bush in clusters; all over the place with water almost to our waists. With slips, cuts, scrapes, climbs, falls, it was unreal, but again we managed.

Do you know what it is like falling, and the only thing you have to grab onto is devil's club? Well I'll tell you, very sore and painful! We plunged on, mile after mile, as tree branches were swinging back in our faces. Dry cedar sticking to our sweating bodies, as our bodies itched from the irritation.

As we were coming to a beach area, Darryl took a fall and sprained his knee. Our clothes were almost in shreds, and we were bleeding constantly on our arms, legs, and faces. Some cuts were quite bad, and should have had medical attention, but the first aid kit that we had received from one of the local sponsors- served the purpose.

Max was miles ahead of us, and the faces of the pedometers were scratched quite bad from the swinging branches, as we had gone through the bush for miles.

Darryl and I just sat on the beach area for five minutes, and just looked at each other, hoping that the rest of the trek was not like this.

We are at Four Mile Creek, and they are building a new park, which should be completed by now. We are just too tired to go on.

I let Darrel rest and then I set up camp by myself. Max had come back and just stayed in the canoe and fished for a while. It took me about two hours to set up camp. I was so sore and tired.

Supper was then started and we had baths in the icy cold waters of Shuswap Lake. When out in the wild, this was the only way of cleansing oneself. At times, the water was so cold that it gave you a headache, but it was still nice getting cleaned up.

Lake walkers on Anstey Arm leg

After two days of hiking the Shuswap Lake Walkers are reported almost up to Cinnemousin Narrows. Indications are they are now on the first leg of the Anstey Arm circuit.

The walkers are Dan Goodale and Darrel Kelly, who left Salmon Arm Marina just after 10 a.m. Saturday. They could be up to a month or five weeks on the trail as they attempt to settle for all time the generations-long controversy over the length of the Shuswap Lake shoreline.

Estimates over the years have ranged from as low as 400 miles to 1,100 and more. But Kelly and Goodale hope to provide more than just estimates as each is carrying a pedometer which, they say, have been checked for accuracy.

Accompanying the two hikers is Max Wilde, who is transporting camping gear and a month's supplies by canoe.

Reports indicate Wilde found it tough going over the weekend as he battled strong winds and heavy wave action which resulted in him reaching Sicamous Sunday about half an hour behind the walkers.

DEPARTURE

Chamber of commerce president Neville Hutton and a handful of interested citizens were on hand for the start of the trek Saturday morning. The start was delayed about 10 minutes as Mayor Margaret Lund had indicated she would be there, but eventually the hikers decided to set off without the civic farewell.

They are marking fence posts, stumps and trees along their route with fluorescent paint to prove their presence and are also hoping to have cottagers and passing boaters sign a paper to verify their presence at a given place at a given time.

This, they say, will serve as further confirmation of their accomplishments and, they hope, help them win a listing in the Guinness Book of Records as the first persons to have hiked completely around the lake.

As another proof of passage, and a bit of an experiment in currents, they also plan to drop occasional notes-in-bottles into the lake. People finding such bottles are being asked to turn them in to the chamber of

Lake walk

Continued from page 1

commerce office in Salmon Arm, along with advice as to the time and location of finding.

Stamp collectors are also getting into the act. Printed envelopes marking the trek have been prepared and will be duly postmarked. Anyone interested in this aspect should contact Tony Wawrzyniak at Box 87, Salmon Arm.

TOUGH GOING

Wawrzyniak was one of those on hand to see the trio off on Saturday, and the following day he joined them for part of their hike.

He reports they reached Canoe at 12:40 p.m. Saturday and carried on to camp overnight at Annis Bay. He caught up with them at 10:55 the next morning, about half a mile east of the tunnels, and hiked with them to Sicamous, which they reached about 1:15.

As an indication of the rough going, Wawrzyniak reports during part of that stretch, with rock face rising steeply from the lake, they stuck to the shoreline and at times were wading chest-high in water.

In Sicamous, he said, the trio contacted tugboat skipper Gordon Mackie who agreed to keep an eye on them during his daily trips up lake, and to convey messages as required.

Wawrzyniak says the "game plan" is to walk until 5 p.m. each day, then make camp and, in the evenings, write up a daily journal which will later serve as a complete record of the journey and the walkers' observations.

He says the trio also hopes boaters will keep an eye out for the red canoe and stop to visit and check the hikers' progress.

When supper was finished, Darryl and I worked on our wounds. We both had quite a few scrapes and scratches. I put a bandage around Darryl's knee that he had sprained. He wasn't in much pain at first, but as the night went on, his knee started to swell. You could now tell that Darryl was in pain.

Max, who had been doing some fishing, came in and gave me a hand to help put Darryl in the tent. The night was coming to an end, and today was definitely one of our toughest days. We had some company from the people who were building the park at Four Mile Creek. They only stayed for about one hour, as it was getting very dark once again. We gave them verification slips to send in to prove our progress. We had fun with them and enjoyed their company.

It was once again time to hit the hay. Max took the tape recorder into the tent. Darryl just lay there moaning in pain. I layed in the middle and just did some thinking. After about an hour of lying in the tent, Max and I heard loud noises. We listened closely, and this time we knew what was outside; they were bears. We could even see them with the moon silhouetting on them.

They were close to the tent, and once again we were afraid. The feeling that you get when you are walking all day, and you have to keep looking behind you because you think that there is something there- is quite eerie, let alone confrontational. It is most fearful when you are walking through the woods.

Most of the time it was impossible to even carry a rifle. You get used to it after a while, but what an excitement it is that runs through your body. I peeked out the back window to estimate the distance between us and these beasts. Suddenly, Max turned the tape recorder on full blast, and David Bowie was playing. I think I jumped right out of my skin. Not only was I thinking about the bears outside, but that almost gave me a heart attack.

The bears took right off, and me, well, I shook for about an hour. Max was laughing his head off. Darryl didn't seem to care what was happening. He was in too much pain. That was the final incident before day four came to a close.

What was tomorrow to bring with Darryl's knee the way it was? If it isn't healed by tomorrow, then we will have to wait for it to heal. Even if it takes a week, we'll wait. We could let Max walk and Darryl canoe until his knee gets better.

We are also conforming to Guinness Book of World Records rules, and it is just not possible to do that. Darryl also had too much pride and we all have our own jobs to do.

I slowly slipped into the twilight zone. It appeared that the tape recorder had scared the bears off for the remainder of the night.

DAY 5

This was now our fifth day out, and we were still camping at Four Mile Creek. Darryl's leg was still bothering him, so we took this opportunity to organize our supplies, rest, and give Darryl's leg a chance to heal. We walked around and did some exploring. As we explored the area, we found some wood and made Darryl a homemade crutch. Darryl laughed at first and then found it to be useful.

Max and I continued to do some exploring, and came across this old cabin in the woods. Someone had named this cabin the 'friendship cabin', and it was really quite original. There was no door to the cabin, and inside the walls- there was names written all over them. Probably names from the people that had come across it. This cabin was strange and we didn't know who it belonged to. We started back toward our camp and ran into Darryl, who was trying out his new crutch. He too, was impressed with this cabin in the middle of nowhere.

If you go up Anstey Arm, head toward Four Mile Creek, and stop to see it- you won't see the cabin from the lake, but take the time to try to find it. It's worth checking it out. We then walked back to camp and started supper.

It was our first time to eat fiddle heads. Fiddle heads are a type of plant that resembles a fern. It has a fibrous root. Some fiddle heads can be poisonous, unless boiled to get rid of any toxins. The leaves from the plant curl from the tip up. When prepared and cooked properly, the plant tastes like spinach.

We also had vegetables, as well as our first catch of fish that Max had caught. It sure was a nice supper. After supper was over, it was time to collect wood before it got too dark.

The wood was damp from the rainfall we have had in the past few days. Rummaging through the pile; we managed to retrieve enough dry wood for our needs. We also found out why we had bears last night. There were a lot of skunk-cabbage plants all over back in the woods, and the bears just love skunk-cabbage. We got our fire going, and Darryl's knee seemed like it was getting better.

It seemed like a wasted day, but we certainly needed the rest. My legs were badly gouged, and the black nats seemed to thrive on the blood that was trickling from the cuts. At one point, a black nat had bit me right on one of my cuts, and when I went to scratch it- I tore the cut open again.

As the fire was crackling, I sat and viewed the beautiful scenes of the Shuswap. I was deeply impressed, and sat out for hours. One more gulp of that beautiful fresh air, and listening to all the nights' sounds before retiring to the tent. Max and Darryl had also turned in as the fire was starting to burn out.

The supplies were now organized and packed up tight for the night. No bear tonight, as I feel asleep. In the middle of the night, Darryl woke me up to tell me that he would be able to walk tomorrow. That sure was good news. Max couldn't sleep all night. He tossed and turned and kept Darryl and I awake half of the night. We are hoping for a better day tomorrow.

DAY 6

At the beginning of our sixth day we could hardly wait to get started. We were up earlier this morning, and ate breakfast by 7:15 a.m. We then took our usual two vitamins, and set off by 8:00 a.m. sharp. It was already starting to get hot out, and we had no choice but to wear long sleeved shirts in order from keeping the branches from cutting us anymore. It was very hard to walk in the hot temperature, feeling cooped up. The cuts on our arms, face, and legs were still fresh, but signs of healing could be seen. They sure ached quite a bit.

We have gone our furthest day today. Twenty miles and our feet sure feel it. Our hiking boots haven't been dry for two days, and it is very hard to walk in them when they are wet. Our blisters are always being irritated, and don't seem to ever heal. It is very painful walking with open blisters. You can already see the toll that the hiking boots are taking; slices and scrapes could be seen all over them. It has been another rough day with rocky terrain, and low lying bush. We estimate that we have been sweating about two pints of water per day. We are each carrying a collapsible cup so we can have access to water as we need it.

There was no one around to hand out questionnaires to, so we are taking pictures of our checkpoints to prove our progress. Approximately two miles from Broken Point, we were faced with sheer cliffs to overcome. These cliffs seemed about two hundred feet high. We climbed up on an angle, and had to stop half way to take a rest. Then, totally exhausted, we climbed and climbed our way. With slips and slides, and dirty faces from the dirt and dust, we clung on tight to make it to the top of this geological nightmare. Once on top, we had to walk another half a mile before we could start to come down. The view from here was absolutely breathtaking. You could see for miles

.

Our fingertips were worn and splitting, from grasping onto the jagged rock forms that we had to use to pull ourselves up this huge cliff. It wasn't as bad going down. We had to be careful not to slip and lose our balance. It was scary because sometimes we would slide quite far going down, and seemed to pick up speed doing so. If you lost control, it could have been fatal.

We named this mountain 'Challenger's Feat', and we were glad that we succeeded in defeating it. Now back to the rocky shoreline again, as we were nearing Broken Point to set up camp for our sixth night.

It was another day with some rainfall, but the majority of the day was very hot and around eighty degrees. It was just unbelievable. We had gone twenty miles, practically nonstop, in long sleeved clothing. It felt great reaching an area where we could stop and set up camp.

The tent is drying out now from the rainstorm that had occurred today. We walked through the storm earlier, determined to make better mileage, and it paid off. The tent hadn't been covered in the canoe. Max is getting more tanned instead of being sun burnt. We sure could go for a cold beer right about now. We were now camping directly across from Pete Martin Creek, and hope to make it to the narrows tomorrow.

So far, we have seen lizards, rock spiders, snakes, chipmunk, squirrel, hawk and crow. Let's not forget bear and more bear. We had more fish again today, and Max is getting better at choosing the right bait. Just after eating and washing out dishes, we saw our first moose. It was in the middle of the water swimming, but didn't seem to know where it was going. We followed it to make sure it got out of the water safely.

I had heard about some moose that try to make it across a river, and end up drowning. This moose was not only a sight to behold, but it was also the first moose that Darryl had ever seen. It was soon off into the woods, and we could not see it anymore.

Night time was once again closing in on us, and it was time to load the rifles, and put them in the tent. The bonfire was lit, and we were just too tired to stay up. We always tried to light a big bon fire before going to bed to keep the animals away. The supplies were tucked away in the canoe, and we pulled the canoe on shore. Night all, and we were all fast asleep.

About two o'clock in the morning; I was awakened by loud noises and footsteps. I woke Darryl and Max up immediately after I was sure it was another bear. Darryl listened, and seemed to think that it was a chipmunk. Max never commented. Again, the same feeling running through our bodies was unreal. Is this where my life ends? Keeping cool and calm were just some of the thoughts that are going through your head at the time. The scary thing is that you don't know what kind of bear it is. Is it a grizzly, brown or black bear?

I peeked out of the tent and saw two large black bear. I thought I had woken up right away but I guess I hadn't, because they were already into our supplies.

We normally leave the canoe anchored about five feet out into the water, but we were so tired from the days trek that we thought we would have no problem leaving the canoe on shore.

The bears were making very loud noises as they rampaged through our supplies. Luckily, the rifles were in the tent, because that was the first thing that I grabbed. We kept cool, but also very tense.

The three whistles that we carry on us was the first attempt to rid the bears. On the count of three, we all blew our whistles at once. These bear must have been starving because they would not leave. Now we were all really scared.

We continued to make loud noises, but they still wouldn't leave. It is very frightening, when you hear the sound of the bears coming from the woods at night, especially when it is absolute quietness.

The eerie crunching of the wood as it gets closer to you is very frightful. More bear were coming from the mountain, and we had nowhere to go.

As I crept out of the tent, Darryl and Max, followed me with flashlights. The rifle is a .22 semi-automatic, and holds seventeen rounds of ammunition.

I fired sixteen rounds simultaneously into the water, only because the water with the mountains in the background would act as a loud echo.

Two bears left the scene, and I had to use the seventeenth bullet to scare the remainder off. What a loud echo it was. They sure were stubborn. Had we not of had the rifle, I don't know how we would have gotten rid of them.

Normally, black bear will scare easily, and fear you right away. But these ones didn't. We were all standing close to the tent, when Darryl and Max slowly faced their flashlights at the canoe.

The canoe was overturned, and we estimated three bags of supplies were missing, and the remainder of the bags were torn apart. What a mess.

The rifle was loaded again, as we checked the aftermath of their presence. I'm sure we were all shaking for a few hours. Our supplies were shortened, and we will try to track some of them down in the morning.

We never slept the rest of the night at all. The bear came back later, rubbing against the tent, freaking us out, but left soon after on their own will.
This was another frightful experience of the Lake walkers.

DAY 7

This morning, just before breakfast, we tried to track down some of our supplies. Which direction do you go in to start to look, we weren't sure, so we covered a small but wide area in the bushes behind our tent. We came up with nothing. It was only day 7, and already we had to ration the remaining supplies. We felt like crying knowing that the remaining supplies would make it nip and tuck to the end.

One more attack like last night, and how were we to continue. This was also a lesson to us to hang out food, bury our empty tins and leave the rest of our supplies out in the water, like we had done, since beginning this trek. I don't think we will ever forget this ordeal. We talked about what had happened, and then, tore down camp to continue on. I remember just wanting to get away from the spot. We are looking forward to reaching the narrows, and then beginning Seymour Arm.

Anstey Arm was definitely a nine on a scale of one to ten for toughness. Deep inside, Anstey Arm will hold a lot of memories for me. Today was to be a six-mile day to the Narrows, and actually our first easy day (if ever there was an easy day). It was about ninety degrees out, and the sun was beating on us as we continued a long rocky six miles. It was so hot that I had to put a damp shirt on my shoulders to keep from burning.

Sweat was teeming down our faces once again. Max could hardly stand it to canoe. His legs were bright red from the continuous rays of the sun, beaming down on the same spot all the time. He had no escape and was at the mercy of the sun.

We had a few minor cliffs along the way in the six miles, but nothing like what we had already covered. As we neared the corner of the Narrows, we all looked at each other and smiled. We had made it. All the way from Salmon Arm Marina, in Salmon Arm to Sicamous, then up to the tip of Anstey Arm, (at one point, looking over at the Narrows) wondering, when we would get over there to set up camp, and here we were.

We felt like we had already accomplished something. It was still early in the day, but we weren't about to continue on and pass up sleeping in the cabins that are located at the Narrows.

The first thing we did was to take off our hiking boots and hang them out to dry. Out of seven days, our boots have only been dry for one day. We didn't have to set up the tent because of the cabins that are located on this site, and that was fine with us. Our cuts from the other day were healing quite well now, as we started to relax, and realize how far we've gone.

By mid-afternoon, trouble had arrived. It was a little pest, a black bear cub. What a nuisance it was. It kept coming toward us. There were people barbecuing who also saw the critter. This bear was about a year old, and I figured that maybe its Mother had just left it. The bear looked in rough shape, and had patches of fur missing from its body. It was just wandering around doing what it wanted.

Nobody was really afraid of it, but as it got closer to us; we climbed up on one of the picnic tables to create a gap between us and it. I had picked up a rock as I climbed on top of the picnic table, and when the bear got too close, I threw the rock at it.

The bear took off and went and bothered other people. You have to be careful in case the bear is facing starvation. A park warden was contacted from someone in a boat. When the park warden arrived, he trapped the bear and shipped it to another area of the lake. We started to wind down a little after the warden took the bear away and reflect on the trip so far.

So far on this trip, the scenery has been awesome; mountain after mountain overlapping each other, you wonder where all the water goes. The beauty of the trees and forests is amazing, and it is so quiet at night. It is so beautiful sitting and listening to the sounds of the loons as they talk to each other. It sure is hard to beat. Every night, I sat out before sundown, and I took photographic pictures in my mind of the beauty that I saw.

Every picture should be a postcard. As I was sitting and entering my diary, a barge, fully loaded, was heading in the direction of Sicamous. I could see all the houseboats slowly floating by off into the distance. This is an artist's paradise. It was so beautiful, laying down and looking up to watch the clouds form into different shapes. The air was so clean and fresh too. I always enjoyed the sounds of the small waves hitting the shore. I found that relaxing. Some people in a green boat were passing us, and beeping their horn and waving to us because they realized that we were the Lake walkers.

We still have a long way to go, but the further we got the more inspired we would get. I could see the finish line every time I closed my eyes. We were three determined young men. We were learning many things on this incredible journey that would make us better people, when we were done.

We were still bathing in extremely cold waters of the Shuswap, but none of us seemed to mind.

Our feet and legs were covered with bites from the black nats that have been bothering us. When we had woken up the other day, there were more than one hundred of them in the tent. They were so small that they crawled right through the screening of the tent. A black nat is like a black fly, but smaller with sharper teeth.

Our feet were sore and blistered, but we were looking forward to tomorrow. Max had put about an inch on his arms from rowing so far, and his burns were turning into a tan. The boots were dry now, and ready for more work tomorrow. Now I know why Stanley Foy loved living out here. It was so fresh and beautiful. You would live an additional twenty years. Now another sound as the fire that Max lit was starting to crackle behind us, and the smell of open campfire lingered in the air.

Yes, a person can do a lot of thinking out here. If only each day was fifty hours long. It was just starting to get dark now, and the sounds of little animals could be heard. I was watching a hawk fly overhead to warn us that his young were nearby. We are learning to appreciate these things. We were sitting, waiting for the lighthouse to start flickering like a candle as it got darker and darker. This was also another beautiful sight.

This is the home for wildlife. It should be theirs, they own it, and we are just intruders. The amount of driftwood that we had seen up to this point was unreal, and the amount of rock was unbelievable. We had continued to pass out as many sighting forms as we could.

We realized that our supplies were cut short, but we knew we were going to make it. We were well aware of the rocky shoreline ahead of us, and knew that we had to plunge on and on in order to complete this task, no matter how tough the terrain was.

Max, he deserves so much credit, for his canoeing. I cannot explain how important his job was. Max had only one paddle now. The other one was lost in a frequent storm. Max said he will use a two-by-four if he has to.

We enjoyed the remainder of the night and were looking forward to Seymour Arm tomorrow. We have now been gone for one full week.

DAY 8

We woke up to the rain this morning, and cooler temperatures. Our clothes were damp and would stick to your body as you put them on. We had a quick snack, and started off right away. We couldn't have lit a fire if we wanted to, and because of the rain we were forced once again to put on our ponchos. I was shivering from the cool breeze hitting my clammy skin.

Darryl was bundled up well, and Max canoed all through the storm. While walking on this rocky shoreline with wet boots; it made it almost impossible not to slip. What a challenge it was to keep your balance. So much for dried boots, they are drenched again. We knew we had to do at least fifteen miles today, so we picked up our stride during the storm.

The rocky terrain today was somewhat different. The rock seemed to be loose, and it was difficult to get proper footing. The constant pounding of your feet into the rock made your knees sore, and the sharpness of some of the rock would cut into your ankles just above your boot line, as your foot would sink down between the rocks.

Along our route today, we spotted plenty of bear droppings on rocks which informed us of only one thing, there could be bear around. As Darryl and I were approaching this high mountain, Max spotted a large cat, probably a mountain lion, so we were extremely cautious.

During the storm, we walked mile after mile, and got completely wet, in spite of wearing the ponchos.

Trees and bush, flush with the edge of the water, we marched our way through. We both fell numerous times, and one time I slipped and fell in the water, right up to my waist. Fortunately, only more cuts and scrapes.

The hiking boots are practically useless when wet. As well as the mountain lion, we also saw a deer and lots of pheasants. The forest here seems to be all rotted. You couldn't rely on a tree to grab onto, if you were falling; the tree would go with you.

We have gone nineteen miles today, and have set up camp at Beach Bay. About three miles from where we were, there was a spot where we were going to camp, but it appeared as though someone had left in a hurry. They had left their kettle, and their tent was torn apart. As we inspected the site, we found piles and piles of bear patties all over the place. That was the reason why we decided to camp at Beach Bay.

We sure wished we could still spray paint our route, as it seemed as though we hadn`t run into too many people since Broken Point. We have gone more than one hundred miles so far, and we sure felt it. Bottles containing notes were dropped in the water by Max today at different points. The notes in the bottles had our location and the date that the bottles were dropped off. These were dropped off, not only for people to find them and report them to the Chamber of Commerce, but would hopefully act as a part in history, if one was to be found years or decades later.

Once camp was set up, Max and Darryl were trying to find some dry wood to light a fire, while I was entering my diary again. The scenery had changed somewhat, and the sun is now behind us. To the right of where I was sitting; was a huge waterfall off in the distance, and the mountains surrounding the waterfalls seemed to have been cleared.

Maybe there was a logging camp or something. The higher level is still snow-capped. The mosquitoes seem to combat the brisk breezes just to get at you. I think they work with the Red Cross, because they take a pint of blood every time. Our feet are sore, and our fingertips are still burnt from wearing them down on sharp rock that we needed to clutch onto to get by some of the obstacles.

We are scared sometimes, but the willingness and courage of all three of us defeat the fear. I'll tell you one thing as I'm sitting here, and I surely mean it; is that it really is hard trying to get into the Guinness Book of World Records. No matter what you do to try and get in, believe me, it's going to be tough.

You could see the toll that the walk had taken on both Darryl and I at the end of each day. Our clothes were soaked with sweat and our hair was drenched. We were glad when it was time to set up camp. As soon as you would wash up and change your clothes; it seemed to bring you back to life.

It was a hard average ten-hour day. Your body was in more than one hundred positions. It wasn't just walking. It was putting up with everything; the hot sun, cold rain, sweating all the time, devils club, and mosquitoes every night. Always hoping you don't slip on a certain rock, thus threatening your life or afraid at night because of bears, and during the day always looking for wildlife as you are walking.

Max's canoeing so far had been superb. He knew when to come close to shore and when not to. At first, we worried that maybe we should have an outrigger attached to the canoe, but Max insisted that was like having training wheels on a bike. Canoeing is his job, so we kept quiet. Now I know why Max has managed quite well.

There wasn't much sense lighting a fire tonight, as Max and Darryl couldn't retrieve any wood. Besides, it was lightening out with loud thunderstorms, and continuous drizzle that would have made the fire smolder. We all stayed in the tent and listened to a tape on the tape recorder. It was uncomfortable with the dampness, but this was to be our best night's rest since starting this trip.

DAY 9

Today we had rough goings the minute we started off toward Seymour Arm. We had to climb this huge mountain to pass the shear rocky face of it. There was a lot of bush along the way, and plenty of devils club. It started to rain, and we are now drenched yet again. We were just so hot from walking that we let it pour on us. Max had to pull over for a few minutes to let the strong, Hercules-type winds blow over, then it was back to rowing again.

We slipped and slid over the wet and rocky terrain, and added a few more cuts to the list. We then ran into a marshy area, with mud and shrubs to content with. After that, it was three miles of walking in sand. Toward the end of Seymour Arm, I saw a moose. I was making my way through a marsh with bulrushes towering over my head. As I was slowly wading in the water, pushing the bulrushes back with my hands to see where I was going, I noticed that I was coming to a clearing.

As I parted the final bulrush (almost like peeking through a stage curtain), there it was, this huge moose. It looked at me and I looked at it, both the moose and I took off in opposite directions. I was yelling and screaming. I think I was walking on water, as I made a mad dash to the shore. I could hear my heart pound, and thought that it was going to pop right out of my chest. I was quite a ways ahead of Darryl, so he didn`t even see what had happened.

At the end of Seymour Arm, there were five little creeks to cross. We board walked the logs that would lead us across. Then it was into a farmer field, as we passed the last stretch at the end. What a mess that was. I was again ahead of Darryl at this point only because of his ailing knee.

Everywhere that I would walk, I would disturb animals that were on this farm. I was sure the farmer would come out with a shotgun. We would seem like we were prowlers. Step after step, you could see geese flying away making all sorts of noise. I could hear the chickens running around, ducks quacking, pigs squealing, and cows mooing.

In a distance, we spotted chamois cattle (bulls) near the front of the farmers' house. There was a whole herd. I knew that this could have been trouble. Not only did we disturb these animals, but if these beasts charged us or took off, there could be a stampede.

I shouted for Max to canoe to the house, and get the farmer. Max also knew that they would charge him, so going to the house was out of the question. We waited excitedly for Darryl to catch up. Darryl was also surprised. After we tried to devise a plan, we realized that we really had no choice but to continue past these cattle.

The man of the house must have been out, because he would have surely heard all the noise by now. We moved slowly past these beasts, by hugging onto the surrounding, dilapidated fence with caution, each step of the way.

After all of that tension, it was time for a deep breath and a sigh of relief. Max was out in the canoe, laughing his head off, trying to send the bulls after us.

REPORT ON SHUSWAP WALKERS FROM SEYMOUR ARM

At 3:30 p.m. Sunday, May 27, the 'Walkers' arrived at Daniels' Store and Marina at the very end of the Seymour Arm branch of the Shuswap Lake.

While looking wet and muddy from rain earlier in the day, they were obviously cheerful and in good spirits. They planned on camping the night on the sand point at Silver Beach Campsite at Seymour Arm. They enquired about type of shoreline: rock bluffs, etc., they could expect on the rest of their journey.

Up-to-date they reported catching two fish, encountering bear, moose and Charolais cattle, all requiring some respect in passing.

Once, the canoeist was escorted by Canada Geese with their goslings. He appeared to be having a more scenic adventure.

Best of luck to the three of them.   (submitted)

We then ran into a gentleman and asked him how to get to the town. "This is the town", he said. This is "Seymour Arm". We laughed, as we expected something like Salmon Arm. He said there were about twelve families living there. There is also a small logging camp at the end of Seymour Arm.

Seymour Arm is enclosed by mountains. It has a floating store-marina combination. The few people there are very friendly. There are plenty of trees, and also a hotel. It was very quiet, and very few people have hydro. The ones that do live here; pay dearly for it. Most of the dwellings are propane heated. There is a little inlet, where houseboats travelling up to Seymour Arm, can dock. We were located at a park called Silver Sands Provincial Park. We had set up camp here.

After setting up camp, we went to the store-marina to talk with the people and hand out a sighting form. It was neat walking on this pier type of a dock, and was going into the store. The people wished us well, and back to our campsite it was. It sure was quiet and peaceful here.

Max caught yet another fish, so we knew what we were having for supper tonight. It was about to rain, so I was going to retire to the tent, when Max started playing the mouth organ. So I stayed out and entered my diary again.

The forest here is beautiful. Darryl and my pedometers are dead on accurate. You could see the wear on the canoe. Max's canoeing has still been superb, and Darryl's walking was getting better every day. His knee should be healed by tomorrow.

As I was sitting looking at the mountains, you could see the clouds hovering below the mountain tops, just floating. There was also an older, heavy piece of equipment sitting off in the distance. It sits idol like a monument, probably been here for years. You could see all these streams running down from the mountains and into the lake. No wonder the water was cold.

When I turned and looked toward the Narrows, the sky was very grey, and it looked like it was pouring hard. It was just drizzling where we were. The water here is very calm and still. Max is praying it will stay that way for tomorrow. We sat around talking for quite a while, and just enjoying the beautiful scenery.

Off in the distance, we could see a bridge on the other side of the Arm, but couldn't quite make out what it was for. Max played the tape deck each day as we plunged on and on. He believes it made us walk further and you know, I think he's right.

The rain started coming down harder now, and Max had just finished playing the mouth organ, so I retired for the evening.

DAY 10

We decided that today; we were going to rest from our long journey. Our clothes were hanging out to dry on our makeshift clothesline. They had been so wet from the past couple of days, as we had been faced with heavy rains. We were surprised today, as Tony showed up for a visit. He caught the ferry from Sicamous, and brought us out some Army Cadet rations to help us because of losing some of our supplies to the bears back at Broken Point.

Tony had heard about the bear attack, and knew that we would be limited for food. These rations of squeezable cheese in toothpaste-like tubes, as well as the small facial powder tins of pate will keep us going. Tony was a really nice caring person. He spent a couple hours with us as we went over the map with him, and showed him some of our war wounds. I read the diary to Tony, and he seemed to really enjoy it.

Tony is a very fit man for his age, even though he always smoked those long skinny cigarettes called 'More'. Tony left us around one thirty in the afternoon. We then sat around and talked about how nice it was of Tony to come all the way from Salmon Arm, and catch a ferry in Sicamous, to Seymour Arm. Like I said, I admit Tony was in good shape, but he was pushing eighty years of age.

As usual, it began to rain again, so I strolled over to the store-marina to chat with Alf Daniels the owner, for a bit. I was enquiring about shoreline up ahead.

The rest of the night was a quiet one. We lit a fire, and compared our wounds similar to how Quint and Hooper did on the movie Jaws. We were sore all over, but yet we were becoming stronger physically. We stayed up until ten o'clock before turning in.

DAY 11

At the beginning of today, we started our routine very slow. Breakfast was cooked at about eight o'clock. We had juice, toast, and red river cereal. We took turns cooking breakfast and washing the dishes. After we were done eating breakfast, we would wash the dishes by scooping some sand in the dish, add a little bit of water, and then swish it around. The grit from the sand and weight of it would act as a scouring pad, and made it very easy to clean the dishes.

By the time we packed up our camp and had our two daily vitamins, it was nearly ten o'clock. We are heading toward the Narrows on the other side of the lake. The Narrows is the center part of the four arms of Shuswap Lake. Picture it as the center of the letter H. It wasn't far since leaving our camp spot, that we were faced once again with more obstacles.

We had to cross this wide stream. The stream wasn't too deep, but it meant getting another soaker. From this stream, it was clawing our way through bush for about a mile or two. We then came to Seymour River. According to Guinness Book of World Records, Seymour River is noted for having some of the strongest currents in the world. I believe they have been recorded at eighteen miles per hour in some areas of the river. I could tell just by looking at the swiftness of the river, that there would be a problem crossing it.

I started off cautiously, and the minute I had both feet in the water; the strength of the rapid water forced me to take a fall. I got completely wet from head to toe. I tried several times to get across, but fell every time, so I decided to go up the river about one hundred feet, where I finally found a spot where I could cross.

While I was making it across, Darryl had tried his luck at the same area that I had just tried, and he wiped out a couple times before following the route that I had took. We had to change our clothes completely, as we were soaked from the head down. When we changed into dried clothing, and decided to put on a pair of gloves.

The next stretch of shoreline was all bush; right up to the edge of the water. At times, we had to walk in the water to get past the bush and dead fall that laid in our way. We went seventeen miles this day, and had scratches on our faces, and torn clothing from the trees and bush. Max had good canoeing today.

Darryl and I saw another black bear and two beaver as we were walking. We also saw a bald eagle and several hawk. It seemed like a lonely day. It was very quiet. All you could hear was the pounding of our hiking boots making contact with the ground. We found a spot to set up camp today at Encounter Point, better known as Five Mile Creek.

The scenery here wasn't as nice as what we had seen so far on this trip. There were a lot of trees and the mountains were like rolling hills. We had hundreds of mosquito bites, and our hiking boots were drenched again as. Before we left on this journey, someone said that our boots wouldn't have a mark on them by the time we completed this trek.

So far the bottoms of our boots are worn somewhat, and the sides are cut quite badly. The hiking boots are 'Vasque' hiking boots, and they should last the remainder of the trip. Seventeen miles is a long way to walk, especially when the shoreline is as rough as it is around Shuswap
.

Our legs are swollen from the pressure that is put on them. Our fingertips continue to be worn and split from the jagged rock. Camp was set up again. It sure is nice when Max sets up camp for us, and especially when he catches supper too.

His canoeing is expected to get tougher in the next few days. We are camping almost at the Narrows, where there is a huge boon of logs floating in the water. We are pleased to be at camp, and rest our feet.

The breezes were starting to get cooler now, and chills were running down our spines as we watched boats way off in the distance. We were quite away out in the wilderness. I entered my diary again, and took in the quietness of the evening.

DAY 12

This morning we were awakened by the sound of a boat coming closer toward us. As the boat came closer, it pulled up to shore. It was a Conservation Officer. His name was Russ, and Russ wanted to know what happened at Broken Point regarding the bear attack. Apparently, somebody had said that we had shot a bear. It was Russ' job to investigate such a complaint. I assured Russ that every shot was fired into the water, and I wouldn't want to hit one anyways, it might make them mad.

We spoke with Russ for about an hour, and he had asked if we would turn our .22 rifles into him, so that people in town would know. He said then that if there were any further complaints, he would know that they were not true. It was my feeling that had we not have had the rifles at Broken Point; things could have turned out differently than what they had.

It was my decision to keep the rifles, only for our own protection. At least until we came out of the wilderness. Russ understood, and then knew that we were telling him the truth about what happened at Broken Point. He wished us good luck and farewell on his journey.

We started our days walk shortly after Russ left. Again, we were faced with rocky shoreline, and driftwood holding us up. There were also plenty of bushes to slow us down too. We would get trapped between the bushes, like a pheasant. Mile after mile, we went on like this. Our fingertips had broken open again from the razor type rock grips we have to rely on. Blood was trickling from them.

This went on and on, and this was definitely our toughest day, even tougher than Anstey Arm.

We fell, and received more cuts. At times, we had to sidewall the mountains and we hardly had anything to hang on to for support. As we found a reasonably good patch to walk on, we could see the ferry headed for Seymour Arm. As it got closer, the ferry turned toward Max who was canoeing up ahead. We could see the man who ran the ferry give Max a bag.

When we got closer, we could see that it was more supplies. This time, the supplies came from a lady in Salmon Arm. We received the bag but the ladies thoughts were more grateful than the supplies. After talking to Gordon Mackie, owner of the Phoebe Anne, for a short while and giving him a sighting form- we headed out again.

We were making poor mileage because of the shoreline, so we knew we would have to walk a long distance today, if we were to make it to the Narrows. Max went ahead of us, hopefully to set up camp and catch us supper.

It was getting darker now, and our first close call occurred. As I was walking by this mountain with my feet in the water, I pulled on this enormous rock for support. The huge rock started to fall towards me.

The instincts and reflexes in my body threw me back, and I found myself completely submerged. As I was coming up, Darryl grabbed a hold of my hand until I could make it to shore.

We estimated this chunk of rock to weigh around seven hundred pounds. Had I not have had proper footing, I would not have been able to get out of the way in time, and I would have been pinned beneath the icy depths of the Shuswap.

I don't know what was holding the boulder because I hardly pulled on it. I was in shock for a while, but we continued on. All that I wanted to do was find a place to camp. I was extremely shaken, and with Max way ahead of us- I had to continue without a change of clothes. The rubbing of the wet clothing on the inside of my legs was causing a rash to develop.

Our next obstacle was a huge waterfall. The water was just teeming down this waterfall. We managed it and never slipped. My skin was very cold from the cool breezes and the cold water. I was extremely drenched, so it didn't matter to me if I got wet anymore. But Darryl got soaked from this waterfall. That was nothing compared to what we were in for.

It was nine o'clock now, and Max was not in sight at all. The best that we could do was to keep walking until we found Max. We really hadn't much choice because we had yet to find anywhere to camp. Our pedometers, believe it or not, were still recording the same distance. They were a bit weather-beaten, but still accurate.

As we came to a corner, there right in front of us, was sheer rock for a long way. Up in the mountains we went; sweating, as the bugs were just starting their nightly invasion. It was dark by now, and we still had nowhere to set up camp. Where was Max, we thought. Much to our relief, Max had arrived with flashlights for us. Our first question to Max was "where is the end?"

Max informed us that we had a mile to go before we could set up camp. It was around one o'clock in the morning, and we began hallucinating. Our energy level was zero. We only had enough energy left to make it to our campsite.

With insects biting our sweaty necks, and our bodies feeling lifeless, we finally came to where we were for the remainder of the night. We had gone eighteen miles today, eighteen grueling miles to be exact.

Max had a nice fire going, and he had caught yet another fish that he was cooking. We ate, talked for a little, and then just passed out in the tent.

DAY 13

We left our campsite this morning at 9:30 a.m., and again, we were faced with obstacles. Our first four miles were not too bad, but after that we ran into another mountain. This mountain was sheer rock. We looked at each other and took a deep breath before attempting it. Max just didn't know what to think. He said "good luck boys", as he was just shaking his head, wondering how in the world we were going to manage this one.

We started to climb and climb and climb. We were so high, we were praying that the rock that our fingertips were holding onto, wouldn't let go. One slip, and for sure you couldn't come out of it alive. I really mean that. We were about 260 feet high, and nothing to stop us if we fell, but the jagged rock below in the water. Max looked like a florescent dot in the water with his life jacket on. That's how high up we were.

As I watched Darryl attempt to pass this narrow, but steep crevice, I noticed that his footings were starting to give away. As he was pushing on his feet to overcome these obstacles, the pressure from his force caused several rocks to fall like an avalanche.

We were at a level on this mountain where you couldn't turn back because you couldn't turn your body around. Darryl managed, and I knew I had to go next. All the footholds and finger holds that Darryl used were now destroyed. I really don't know how he managed, as there was no possible survival if you fell. How was I going to do it, with no support at all?

I knew I had to make it across this geological fault. I ended up on this ledge about a foot and a half, and found myself slowly slipping off of it. This ledge was the only thing between life and death.

We were both very afraid, but we tried to stay calm, although we knew the chances of making it were slim. All I could see was the water smashing up against the sheer base of the mountain below me. I was trapped, nowhere to go. I was so scared that my body felt weak and lifeless. I had clammy sweat that wouldn't even run down my face. It almost felt easier to jump.

After about an hour of trying to figure out how to overcome this situation, and slipping three more inches to the edge, we decided that we only had once chance left. Here was the situation. I was stuck on this ledge, with jagged rock at my back, curving over my head. A foot and a half ledge, then a 260 foot drop. I don't think I have to explain the feeling, but you have to try to stay calm about it or you would fall.

Several times, Darryl tried helping me but just couldn't. Max was far ahead of us now. Darryl knew how I felt, so we told jokes to each other to try to relieve the tension. Our only chance was for Darryl to climb above me, reach down under the rocks that were covering my head, take wrist upon wrist, and pull me up so I could stand. The rocks that were supporting me were giving way, and it was only a matter of time before they would give out on me.

It was now a race against time. Darryl climbed overhead, and I could see his hand come down. That was the only thing I had to hold onto.

Darryl risked his own life to save both of ours. One slip from Darryl, and we would both fall and have no chance of survival. I didn't want to, but I grabbed Darryl's wrist. There was water flowing out the sides of my eyes, in fear, as I prayed the best prayer I knew. As I grabbed Darryl's wrist, the ledge that I was on collapsed, and plunged to the bottom of the mountain.

Now there was nowhere to put my feet. If Darryl or I let go; that was it. Pulling me up over the curved jagged rock, our hands started to bleed from scraping against the rough edges. We both weren't about to let go though. Four feet later, I had footing as I watched the waves once again as they smashed against this mountain like a Muhammad Ali vs. Joe Fraser rematch.

Darryl and I just lay on the top of this mountain, totally exhausted, and mentally fatigued. What an ordeal, we couldn't believe it. This was a close call, very close, too close!

When we regained our composure, it was now time to go down. It was easier going down and we slid most of the way, being very careful of the drops and gaps that it had.

You can see this mountain as you are coming around the Narrows, and you will probably still see all of our sliding marks that could have ended our lives. This area is called Ruckle Point. The only way we got up and down this mountain safely was with God's help. That, I know for sure.

It was a pleasure getting back to the immediate shoreline again. We then had five miles of smaller cliffs that were also tense at moments. So far on this trek, we consider ourselves very blessed. We have covered every inch of shoreline to this point, and we are determined to put the miles behind us.
Just after Ruckle Point, we came to a better shoreline. It was very good going from there, to where we ended up at Magna Bay.

We had made good time because of the beach. We are so happy to be alive. I had mailed more of Tony's letters, from our checkpoint in Angelmont. Angelmont is a small, but nice community. Most of the people here knew who we were.

We also handed out more sighting forms. We had caught up to Max, and now Max had to catch up to us from Angelmont to Magna Bay, because of the extremely strong head waves. His arms were sore as the day ended.

Camp was set up at Magna Bay. Shortly after setting up camp, someone came out of a house, and tried to scare us off the beach. I guess it was a private beach or something. As soon as they found out who we were and what we were doing, everything was okay. We will leave for Scotch Creek tomorrow.

We are hoping to camp there for the weekend to organize supplies and wash our clothes. We have some rough terrain ahead of us as we get closer to Copper Island. The weather (other than Max's head waves) has been all right. The water is still very cold to bathe in. We are just going to sit around tonight, light a fire, and relax.

I entered my diary again, and then we attended to our wounds once more. We had plenty of cuts and scrapes and some of our older wounds opened up again.

Darryl and I just couldn't get over the situation we were in earlier today that could have easily ended our lives.

I know Darryl has extremely strong forearms, but God must have intervened to give him the extra strength.

How do you pull a one hundred and eighty-pound person up over an overhang? At one point, when the ledge gave way and he had the entire weight of my body to hold onto, he was practically lying on his belly while above me. It definitely was a miracle.

God was definitely with us on this journey!
We enjoyed the remainder of the night, before turning in.

ON WHEELS

If you see the Shuswap Walkers, keep in mind that their food supply is very low. If you can offer them a peanut butter sandwich, they would surely appreciate it. And if you offered them beer or cigarettes, you would be their friend for life.

DAY 14

Before leaving Magna Bay this morning, a lady at the store in town treated us to a home brewed coffee, before leaving for Scotch Creek. Magna Bay is a nice place with plenty of beach. We handed out more sighting forms, and talked to a few people before continuing on to Celesta.

We could only find Celesta by spotting the Bob's Supermarket sign on the shoreline, and followed it to his store. Shortly before spotting the Bob's Supermarket sign, we talked to a gentleman who was retired, and was volunteering to reconstruct parts of Celesta Community Center. He showed us the inside of it. It was huge inside.

After giving him a sighting form, we continued on to Bob's Supermarket. The post office is at Bob's, and this was another one of our checkpoints, so we mailed another set of envelopes back to Tony. We spoke with the owner for a while, and then continued on. We still have a beach to walk on for a while, and you could see Copper Island getting closer. Scotch Creek wasn't far now. We had heard about a few steep cliffs in the area ahead, but they were nothing compared to what we had already tackled.

We came to an area where the water was flush with the road, so we had to take a small stretch of road to pass over the shoreline. Continuing on, people seemed to think that we started out from Salmon Arm Marina, and are heading in a westerly direction. They say we have covered the hardest areas, and should be alright from here on in. Max had another day of strong winds, and rough waters. We had to wait for him twice. We stopped at a store right before Scotch Creek, located on the beach. A lady named Margaret owned it, and bought us all a Pepsi.

We had a laugh with her for a while, then she brought out some up to date paper clippings of us on our trek. We thanked Margaret, and carried on right next door to the park. It was a nice clean park. We were given a spot for camping in the organized campground section. No charge. We were quite happy; at least we were seeing people again.

Because of the location of our site, we had to carry our supplies about a half of a mile. Max set up camp once again. We were happy to have covered most of the rough terrain, at least so far. Darryl and Max did the washing, and I tended to the supplies. I then cooked supper after a fire was lit. We have met three Rangers so far who were quite interested in our trip.

We enjoy it when they come over to chat. It makes us feel good. We are thinking about staying here an additional day, and take advantage of the facilities, some of which we haven't seen for a while. The weather was just beautiful, so I stayed up as long as I could.

We had some company from other campsites, and those people brought over a few beers. I never thought I would miss the taste of a cold beer. I'm sure I squeezed the bottle to the last drop. It was like heaven!

Shuswap Walkers are clipping along

By Sally Scales

Tony Wawrzniak holds a map of Shuswap lake and follows the shoreline with his left index finger, to show how far the Shuswap Walkers have walked. Tony took the ferry from Sicamous on Monday, May 28, and visited the walkers in Seymour Arm.

Darrell Kelly, Dan Goodale, and a canoeist, Max Wilde, left Salmon Arm at 10 a.m. Saturday, May 19, in an attempt to determine the length of Shuswap's Lake's shoreline. Both walkers are wearing pedometers.

On the first night, they camped at Annis Bay; second, Hungry Cove; third, east of Cinnemousun Narrows; fourth and fifth, near Four Mile Creek; sixth, Broken Pt.; seventh, directly across from the Narrows; eighth, Beach Bay; ninth, Seymour Arm; tenth, May 28th, Boy Scout Camp near Wood's Landing.

Tony brought news that a bear had taken most of their food supply at Broken Point, on their sixth night out, so we sent a few rations with Gordon Mackie on his ferry run from Sicamous to Seymour Arm on Wednesday, May 30. The next day, at 4:30 p.m., the walkers phoned the Shoppers' Guide with news that they were at Anglemont Marina, and they thanked all the staff for sending food.

The three young men were in good spirits. They missed two things: beer and Kentucky Fried Chicken.

On Friday, June 1st, they phoned Tony at 10 a.m. from Magna Bay, and said they would be spending the weekend at the Scotch Creek government campsite.

Tony is an experienced outdoorsman; he took many hiking and kayak trips in his native Poland. Now retired, he is keenly following the Shuswap Walkers' adventure. He visited them in Sicamous and Seymour Arm, and this week he will visit them in Sorrento.

"The canoeist has the toughest job," says Tony. "The walkers have it easy. They often have to wait for the canoe if the weather is bad." The canoe is so full of supplies that it cannot carry all three men at once. Where they have to cross a major river, as they will again at Squilax, the canoeist must make two trips to take the walkers across.

The walkers are keeping a daily journal, but they are not releasing any mileage figures. Tony estimates that, at the rate they are going, the shoreline is under 500 miles long.

At the rate they are going, they may be back in Salmon Arm in a week. Be prepared for a "Welcome Home" party when they return!

* * * * * * * * * *

DAY 15

Last night was a comfortable night. A lot of people came in the camp for the weekend. There were sing-a-longs, wiener roasts, and people just gathering at each other's campfires. We felt like celebrities. It was during the night that we decided if our clothes were not dry by the morning than we would stay another night.

When we awoke this morning; it was rather muggy in the tent. I got up and checked our clothes and they were still very wet, so we took the liberty of staying an extra day. We are sure hoping that our clothes are dry by tonight.

We were invited to go to the beach today to see these gas powered airplane competitions, and watch the planes fly around. Another Ranger named Eden came over and chatted with us for a bit. He told us that he just quit smoking. I said he should talk to Darryl and try to get him to quit. Darryl was the only smoker out of us three.

Although it was nice taking the day off; we should have enjoyed this time more, but we were eager to keep going and we wanted to continue on our walk as soon as possible, and put more miles behind us. After the planes had flown around for a while, we went back to our campsite. Darryl went down the nature trail and Max just listened to the tape recorder. I entered the diary again. We handed out quite a few sighting forms to people at this park.

We started another fire as this day seemed short and darkness was closing in. Out came the popcorn, Jiffy Pop to be exact. It turned out good and we enjoyed the taste of it. After the jiffy pop, I wanted to show Darryl and Max how to boil water in a paper bag. They laughed at me, and didn't believe me. I said "if you get a cup ready with a tea bag in it, I will boil the water in a paper bag to fill the cup". They thought I had lost it. You should have seen them laughing. They were laughing so hard that I started laughing too.

When we all calmed down, I said "I'm serious!" Well, I had packed a couple of paper bags before we left on this trip. I went and got one of the bags, and went and saturated the outside of the bag in water. I then put exactly one cup of water inside the bag.

As I gathered the top of the bag together so that the heat couldn't escape, I held the bag just above the flames of the fire. As the outside of the paper bag was drying, the inside water was beginning to boil. Voila! Boiled water for your tea!

Darryl and Max looked like I was some kind of a magician or something. You should have seen their faces. I said that they better be good, or I'll make them disappear.

We were determined to leave in the morning no matter what, so we then went to the registration office of the park to thank them for their hospitality, and for letting us stay there at no charge.

The Shuswap Walkers camped at Scotch Creek government campsite during the weekend, and took time to do their wash.

Darrell Kelly, left, and Dan Goodale, right, are walking around Shuswap Lake to determine the length of the shoreline, and Max Wilde, centre, the canoeist, has the hardest job of the three. He has to paddle a fully-loaded canoe and battle the weather and other boats' wakes.

A report on Monday, June 4, was that the canoe had a one-inch hole, which may slow their progress.

Because of public concern over the guns they were carrying, which would provide no protection from a bear attack, the men sent the guns and ammunition to Salmon Arm.

Marlene Kelf photo

DAY 16

Today was a sunny day. We had a full belly of porridge before saying goodbye to some of the people that we had met. We are seeing more people now as we are heading toward the bridges in Chase. People have been great to us so far, and we really appreciated it. I guess we have covered most of the rough terrain, but we really don't know what is ahead of us.

As we approached Scotch Creek River, there was no sign of Max. We figured that he would be well ahead of us, but we had walked miles without spotting him. This river is about two hundred feet across, and who knows how deep. We waited awhile longer before deciding to walk across it. This time, Darryl, being the taller of us, was choosing to go first. He held his pedometer in his hand, and with each stride, deeper into the water, he would engage the pedometer to record that step.

Deeper and deeper he sank. The water was waist level, than chest level, still deeper until all that I could see was Darryl's head. That was the deepest level in the river. We have walked through every river on this mission, but nowhere near as deep as this one. It was now my turn to cross. I began to sink deeper. As I kept stepping, the water rose to my chin level. I could feel the currents passing by my ankles, like the breeze blowing against my face. The final height of the water was my lip, and I was on my tip toes.

I worked hard to keep my balance, as I held the bag of supplies high in my hand. Any deeper and I would have had to swim. Darryl and I were both drenched again from head to toe, unbelievable, another obstacle that we had overcome. The cool breezes didn't make matters any better. We had goosebumps the size of golf balls.

We were worried about Max. We could feel something was wrong. We started walking again and noticed the canoe up ahead, but no Max. This took our minds off of the chilliness of our bodies. It sure was cold walking in wet clothes with cool breezes. We found the canoe floating in the water. It wasn't even tied to anything. All we cared about was where Max was. Max had been complaining the last few days of the pressures of the trip.

That was when we thought he must have quit. Darryl and I looked at each other and had the same feeling. Could this be true? Right away we checked the canoe to see if his belongings were gone. Everything of Max's was missing. Apparently the pressure of the trip was too much for him.

We couldn't figure out why he wouldn't have left a note or even tie the canoe up. He could have been homesick. I mean, he came out to visit us and ended up coming on this trip. It was Day 16, maybe he thought it would take another 16 days. It is something that we may never know.

Now we were really worried. Not only were we worried about Max, how would we continue? What about the supplies and canoe? The highway was just above us, as the shore ran parallel with the highway. So we looked to see if Max was hitchhiking, yet still, no sign of him.

As we were looking for Max, we spotted a guy trying to get a ride. He looked like he was having it rough. I asked him where he was hiking to, and he said Toronto. We explained about what had happened to our canoeist as best we could, and asked if he would canoe our supplies until we sorted out this problem. He was offered food and shelter in return for his favor. He jumped at the chance. His name was Bill, and Bill canoed to Cottonwood Park while Darryl and I continued walking and wondering why Max had left.

We arrived at Cottonwood Park, and went to ask the people if we could camp on the beach. Bill stayed in the canoe, as we felt uncomfortable by his presence. It just wasn't the same as having Max. No sooner did we get to the office, and we were greeted by a lady. The lady knew nothing about our walk, but her husband who was quick to join her; was right up to date with our progress. They put on supper and offered us a campsite.

Their names are June and Laurie New, and they were extremely nice to us. We talked for about three hours, and then got a tour of the park. Mr. New had lots of antiques lying around.

Bill never had much to say. We set up camp, and because June and Laurie New were so nice to us, we offered them a coffee at our campsite.

Later, we tried to find out more about Bill. It felt strange, sharing the same tent with a stranger, so Darryl and I were very cautious.

It had rained that night, so we laid back and listened to the pitter patter of the rain drops on the tent.

DAY 17

We woke up at eight o'clock this morning and found that we had to patch two holes in the canoe. Somehow, Mr. New had come along and patched the canoe, while Mrs. New brought us coffee and a small bag of supplies. They really enjoyed helping us out, and we couldn't thank them enough. It sure gives you a warm feeling when someone is good to you. We said our goodbyes and headed for the Squilax Bridge.

We explained to Bill- to canoe and wait for us at the bridge and stay close to shore. For starters, we were faced with marsh and bush. It was a long hard plunge as we headed for the forest. Bear patties were all over the place, which really twitched our senses. By this time on the trip, we were used to such things that it didn't really bother us anymore. But we had turned our rifles in at Scotch Creek Provincial Park. We hoped we hadn't turned them in too soon.

We went about three miles through the bush and swampy areas, and after several insect bites, we found Adams River. We backtracked up the river to find a crossing, and found ourselves quite a way up before we could find a suitable place to cross. We crossed the river and continued on toward the Squilax Bridge. We were more worried about Bill taking off on us, than I was the shoreline that we were walking on. He had all the time in the world to just up and go. Our pace was really good, at this point.

We felt good knowing that we were getting closer to the end of our trip. We finally got to the Squillax bridge, and decided to walk over the bridge and down the embankment on the other side.

I saw Bill, as we continued on hoping to make it to Sorrento and meet Tony, as planned. Bill fell way behind and almost tipped the canoe three times.

We knew then that we had to do something in Sorrento. I told Darryl that we would have to backpack the remainder of the trip. Darryl agreed. The shoreline to Sorrento was not too bad, and we were right on time to meet Tony.

When we had a chance, we explained to Bill that if he continued- he would only tip the canoe, and we had too much responsibility with it. I packed Bill some bread and butter, and really thanked him for trying. Bill understood and wished us good luck. It was nice of Bill to try for us, but we really didn't know him, and we did feel uncomfortable.

We then met with Tony and explained what we thought might have happened to Max. We told Tony that we weren't sure where he was, and that we now had to backpack the last leg of the trip. We also told Tony that sighting forms were handed out quite frequently throughout the trip, except in the areas where few people lived.

We started making backpacks out of garbage bags, when we thought of Milt Michaels of the Jock Shop. We got in touch with the Jock Shop, and Milt said, "no problem boys, I will deliver them to you at the Post Office in Sorrento at 10:00 p.m." While we were waiting for Milt to arrive, we talked with Tony a little longer and then walked Tony to the road.

We then met a guy on the beach named Bernie. Bernie offered us a spot on the beach to camp-out, being that it was all private property. We accepted, and set up camp. Later, Bernie came out just as Darryl and I were finishing supper.

He offered us to come inside for a coffee, and meet his Mother and Father in law. Once again, the topic was our journey. We spent three beautiful hours sharing stories before it was time to meet Milt. Milt was right on-time, and he had brought three backpacks to choose from.

We talked with Milt for about half an hour before thanking him once again before heading back to the tent. Milt is incredible, and has also supported us all the way through this trip.

Darryl and I sat up talking for a while, as the cool Shuswap breezes chilled us as they blew by. The lake was rough now, and the mosquitoes were ready for combat again. It was about 11:00 p.m. and our fire was slowly burning itself out, like a gas stove running out of fuel.

We then knew that it was time to hit the sack. Besides, we have had a long hard day. It was chilly tonight. The dampness from our tent and sleeping bags seemed to match the breezes, outside.

FLASH!

The most recent report
from the Shuswap Walkers is that
Max Wilde packed up and left.

The two other men will now
proceed with back packs sent
to them by the Jock Shop

DAY 18

We were up at eight this morning to sort out our remaining supplies. We could only take what we had to in our backpacks. It was extremely difficult to make a decision on what to take. We knew our main necessity was food, but most of our food supplies were canned goods, and they were too heavy and bulky. We still couldn't figure out Max. Maybe it was harder canoeing than we even thought. It must have been too much for him. It was too late now to worry about it. We had to do our best with what we had.

After taking what we could, we gave the rest of our food supplies to some people in a cabin that had some small children. We couldn't stand to see the food go to waste, and no one was home at Bernie's. We headed out with what we could salvage from our supplies. We also had to break in these backpacks. There were several adjustments along the way, as the packs rubbed and marked our shoulders.

Each pack weighed about 68 pounds. It was like someone sitting on your back. Determined to move on and get closer to the finish, we again plunged on and on. Sweat was pouring down us, seeping through our clothes. I think the backpacks were breaking us in. Our shoulders were very sore, and our backs were now in a crouched position.

At the four mile mark on both pedometers (which were still accurate) is when the straps from the backpacks cut their way into our shoulders. We were trying to make Eagle Bay by tonight, and it was still early in the morning. We handed out more sighting forms and dropped off more envelopes at the Blind Bay Post Office.

When something was to be dropped off in a town; one person would go while the other man held onto the pedometer of the man that went into town, thus keeping the measurement of the shoreline as accurate as possible. We continued on after the Post Office, when a mile later, all of a sudden a storm came out of nowhere. It was like a U.F.O. sighting, and we were caught right in the middle of it. This was nothing new for us because on this walk- we walked through many a sudden and frequent storm. Only in this one, our packs would get soaked.

We hadn't packed our ponchos. They were torn apart from the branches, and bush that we had already walked through. We managed to stay as dry as possible, and spotted a Marina up ahead. That's where we headed for shelter. As we arrived at the Marina, it was just teeming out. The rain was running down our faces, like when it rains on the windshield of your car.

We went inside to see if anyone would mind us waiting until the storm let up. Mrs. Lil Howe's of Blind Bay Marina welcomed up. She looked like she could use the company on this specific day. It was a gloomy day. The sky was as grey as it could be. We sat and talked for a while; while the storm raged on. The power went out, and the inside of the Marina began to get cool.

Again, we were chilled to the bones. The boats at the marina were tossing back and forth from the strong winds that seemed to do what they wanted. The storm lasted about two hours before letting up. We decided to head out again and put more miles behind us. Mrs. Howe's is a very nice lady, and we enjoyed her company very much.

Lake walkers on final lap

The Shuswap Lake Walkers team has now been reduced to two for the final leg of the journey.

As of Wednesday night they had reached Sorrento on their round-the-lake hike; which means they only had the south shore to Cinnemousun Narrows ahead before reaching the final pull down the north side of the Salmon Arm of the lake.

Dan Goodale and Darrel Kelly left Salmon Arm May 16 and the time of the progress to date would indicate the shoreline of the lake is not as long as many people had previously estimated.

Max Wilde, who has been accompanying them by canoe and transporting camping gear, left the duo at Sorrento. The rest of the distance they will carry what they need on their backs.

Tony Wawrzyniak of Salmon Arm, who has been keeping in close contact with the walkers, estimates that as of yesterday they had about 80 miles to go. At the rate they've been travelling thus far, he calculates they should reach journey's end by the weekend.

Wawrzyniak reports the walkers are "in good condition and good spirits."

The walkers have so far declined to release mileage figures but if one assumed they have been averaging something in the order of 20 miles a day, indications are the total length of the lakeshore would be some 400-450 miles.

In past most estimates and tourist promotion literature has indicated a shoreline distance anywhere from 700 to 1,000 miles.

It was quite cool outside, but we walked on and on. Through marshes and low lying bush we went chalking up the miles. Up ahead, we could see many rocks and some cliffs, which would be more difficult to get by with backpacks on. Never the less, we had to do it. We were sweating so much, and yet it was so cold out. We kept moving along, making good time. If we had made good time, then we would be able to stop and talk to people, but if we were behind, than a quick hello would be about it.

We heard a voice behind us call us over. It was a lady offering us a coffee and cookies. We really wanted to keep going, but we also didn't want to hurt her feelings. So we stopped and had a coffee with her, her husband and some friends that they had over. Their names were Fred and Tommy Faulker. We stopped to talk with them briefly, had fun, and continued on. That was our last stop of the day before heading for Eagle Bay.

It was getting later now, and the winds were picking up. The winds seemed to throw us off balance as we stumbled over the rough and rocky terrain. The scenery was great, as I kept an eye open for any new cloud-formation that would give us an indication of another storm. We came to a place that said 'Eagle View Resort'. Some people came out to meet us and to take pictures. We were sopping wet from sweat and were very tired. We were informed that we were four miles from Eagle Bay. These people invited us to camp at their place. We again accepted an offer, and set up the tent.

We were invited by the owners; Larry and Pat Moen, to use the facilities. So a hot shower was the first thing on the agenda. The shower was great. I believe this was the first hot shower that we have had so far on this trip. Mr. Moen was doing some repair work on his peer, so Darryl called home to see if anyone had heard from Max.

Max was home, said that the trip was just too much for him and was very sorry. He wished us the best, and couldn't believe that we had made it this far. When Darryl came back and told me, I was relieved that he was all right. Max did a fantastic job for us, and got us through the worst of this trip.

It started raining again while Darryl and I sat out on the picnic table eating our supper.

Mr. and Mrs. Moen must have thought that we were crazy sitting out in the rain, like we were doing. We were just used to it. This was normal for us. Sometimes, even when we were having lunch and it started to rain- we would just continue our meal.

We were already wet anyway. Soon, the cool breezes dried us off.

The day had come to an end. I entered my diary, and we turned in early as the temperature started to decline quite rapidly.

DAY 19

Last night, the temperature took a tumble. It was like being locked in a freezer. I had to breathe into my sleeping bag to stay warm, and sometimes that didn't even help. It was also cold this morning. We tore down the tent and got set for another days trek. Mr. and Mrs. Moen brought out a loaf of Mrs. Moen's homemade bread to take with us. We thanked the Moen's and headed down the old shoreline once again.

Our destination was the Narrows. We started getting used to the backpacks by now, even though it was awkward climbing hills, and walking on slippery rock. The terrain was a little rugged, as we put each mile behind us. There was only one stop today, and that was a lady named Lucy Hack. We had a cup of tea and a brief chat before heading on. After Lucy's, the terrain got rough due to the fact that the water level had risen. Now, in some places, we were in bush.

We had cuts again as we pushed branch after branch out of our way. It was like torture, getting whipped across the face, every time a branch would swing back at you. We were sweating quite a bit again, and the bugs were sticking to our skin. Not to mention- dry cedar again. Our arms were sticky from some sap that had dropped from a tree, and our clothes were getting ripped. The branches would puncture right through the material.

Several times, we got trapped in the bush because of our backpacks. Our pants were soaked again, as we would have yet lower lying bush. We would have to go knee high in water to get around. We would have to do this in many instances, or take your pick and climb a huge cliff instead. These were some of the choices we had to make, but it would still not stop us. We ended up at Wild Rose Resort in Wild Rose Bay.

We went to ask the people how far it was to the Narrows because it was getting dark. Well, if they weren't expecting us. They refused to let us walk any further. Owner Bob Salter insisted that we take a cabin for the night. This cabin was right on the lake. Can you believe it, a cabin overlooking the lake. We were left speechless.

All we wanted was to know how far it was to the Narrows. We never expected at any time that people would be so helpful. That wasn't all that Bob and his wife Dorothy had done for us. As we were inside the cabin setting down our backpacks, Bob came over with a bag of food for supper and for breakfast. It was just incredible.

Bob knew everything that we were doing on this trip, and enjoyed what we were doing as well. Instead of giving us single eggs, he gave us double yolks. We thought, is this what it's like to be in Hollywood or what! All Bob and his wife Dorothy were doing was something they enjoyed, and that was helping someone out. Bob and Dorothy both could see that we were very tired and sore. Mentally and physically, we were still in good spirits.

We chatted for a while and then headed for the cabin for the night. This was to be our first soft bed in 19 days. We ate supper, had a hot shower, and sat back in the peacefulness of this cabin, and relaxed to the delights of modern living. I was sore all over. Darryl went outside for a walk, and I entered my diary once again. The fresh air, and the scenery were enough to put anyone in a joyous mood.

I turned in early this night. Darryl stayed up late. I found it hard to get used to sleeping on something so soft. I had a hard time sleeping, so I decided to stay awake as well. I guess I just wanted to enjoy this cabin as much as possible.

Tonight was a night that we didn't have to worry about anything. We couldn't care less if it rained out, or how cold it was. We were inside and we loved every minute of it. It is now the people from around the lake that are giving us the incentive to continue to the finish.

Shuswap Walkers enjoyed hospitality at Wild Rose Bay

By Sally Scales

Darrell Kelly and Dan Goodale suffered a blow when their canoeist left them at Sorrento. With heavy packpacks and only necessary supplies, the final stretch of their walk around Shuswap Lake, to measure the shoreline, is going much slower.

On Wednesday, June 6th, they arrived at Wild Rose Bay, and Bob and Dot Salter welcomed them to Wild Rose Marina. They gave the boys a cabin and a bed, both luxuries to Darrell and Dan, who had been tenting since they left Salmon Arm May 19th.

The boys had been working "pretty hard," reported Bob, and had cuts, bruises, and were sore, but appeared in good spirits. The next morning, after feasting on a hearty breakfast which included fresh eggs and lots of coffee, and with a supply of cigarettes, the Shuswap Walkers bid farewell to their gracious hosts, then continued on their journey.

DAY 20

This morning, after a hearty breakfast in our cabin, we went to the house for a coffee. Bob said that he had radioed into the town to let people know where we were. Dorothy and her daughter Diane were too busy pricing to strike up a conversation. So Bob made up for the both of them. We chatted a little while then took pictures, and thanked Bob and Dorothy for their hospitality before parting. We also left them a very nice note in the cabin.

We then left Wild Rose Resort, and headed for the Narrows. We are planning on reaching the Narrows, resting up and head for home. As we moseyed along on our way to the Narrows, we were again faced with cliffs, bush and rock. After tackling the huge mossy cliffs, we met a lady named Rose from Calgary. She was having trouble with her dock, so we stopped to repair it for her. Rose was from Calgary, but had a cottage on the lake.

As you have read so far, we have met a lot of nice people who have been good to us, and we appreciated it. It is the nice people that keep us going. We were again, struggling, and sweating to make it to the Narrows by nightfall. It was getting colder out now, and we could see the lighthouse up ahead.

When we had left Wild Rose Resort this morning, Bob and Dorothy had asked us to stop in and see some close friends of theirs. Don and Betty Cowan. Bob said that we would be walking right past their cottage, and described it to us. As we were pacing faster now and the lighthouse was getting closer, we could see Don and Betty's cottage, as described by Bob Salter.

We went right up to the door and sure enough, Betty came right to the door to greet us. Don was fishing, so Betty called Don on their 2-way radio to come back to the cottage. Just as Don was answering Betty's call, he caught a five pound rainbow trout.

We were stopping at the Narrows to set up camp, and Don and Betty's was only about a mile from the Narrows, so we spent a while with them talking and sharing stories. We talked about everything. Then Don and Betty showed us their home that they had built for themselves.

It was just beautiful, and I could tell that they were both very proud of it. You could clearly see all of the work that they had done. Then there was Stamp, Don and Betty's dog. Stamp was a golden retriever, and a very friendly dog with quite the background. Don and Betty are very happy people, and after chatting for yet another hour, we set off but not without Betty packing us a little snack.

Don and Stamp showed us a trail that would help lead us to the Narrows. The path ran flush with the shoreline, so our figure was still accurate. It took us about an hour to get to the Narrows. The walking became very slow. When we arrived, we spotted a cabin at the park. It was just a shell with a concrete floor and a wood stove inside.

This is where we will be staying tonight.

We are going to stay here for a few days to rest up before completing the last leg of the journey. Don had followed us in his boat to the Narrows to make sure we got over some of the cliffs on route.

He was happy to see that we had once again gotten over another obstacle. Two beeps of his horn, and he was off heading back to his cottage. It was getting dark out by now, so we went inside the cabin to unload our backpacks.

The floor would be rough to sleep on, but it felt safe being indoors. I went for a walk down to the water, and sat and stared at all the beautiful scenery. Across from where we were now, was the other Narrows Provincial Park.

We could tell that we have covered a lot of terrain. We felt proud knowing that we were indeed on our last leg of the trip. There wasn't too much else that we could do tonight, because the darkness was upon us now, so we decided to go indoors and rest.

DAY 21

We had a rough sleep from sleeping on the concrete floor inside this cabin. But feeling safe definitely took away any tiredness that we felt. As we opened the door to the cabin, we could see a park ranger, so I went over to speak with him. His name was Al, a very nice man who really enjoyed his job. He said he stops in once in a while to make sure everything is all right.

Al was just getting ready to leave and go elsewhere on the lake, so he wished us luck, and took a sighting form with him. Shortly after Al left, we were faced with yet another pest. It was another black bear cub. It had gotten into our campsite, as well as some girls that were staying in another cabin.

There were about twenty girls from a canoeing group that were out practicing canoeing techniques, when this bear climbed up and entered their cabin through a window to snoop around. Al the ranger had come back because he forgot something, So Darryl, Al and myself were all trying to scare the bear off but the bear was so hungry that he was standing on his own.

I think tonight it is going to really make a move. It comes right up to the cabin, and won't even budge when you try to scare it off. That's how hungry it was. Right now, I'm just worried about the girls. We had heard before leaving for this trip that most troubled bears were trapped and then shipped to Anstey Arm, and set free. I guess we must have passed the area where these bears were set free. This bear is a real nuisance. If nothing is done soon, there could soon be trouble. You could tell that this bear is undernourished.

His ribs stuck-out right through his dull lifeless fur. The ranger is supposed to have a trap coming on Monday, but I think Monday may be too late. We could have a fatality by then. We are leaving tomorrow, and I am thinking of putting a sign up to let boaters and campers know, so that they can be aware of this pest, but I don't want to alarm anyone.

The winds are picking up once again, and it looks like there might be another storm. I am looking right across from where we are located, and it is just amazing, the distance that we have covered to this point. Once again, the scenery is breathtaking. The mountains to the left of me are still snow-capped. This is for sure the most beautiful lake that I have ever seen. In my opinion, Shuswap Lake should be one of the seven wonders of the world.

I can see a plane fly off in the distance. I can tell by the sounds of its motors that it is getting further and further away. Yes, I do think it is going to rain. I have never felt so much at peace with myself, as I have on this trip. During the day it is like terror, hoping that nothing bad happens to either of us. It has been a difficult trip so far, and it has also been very emotional. I don't think that either Darryl or I ever believed it would be as tough as it had been.

Nevertheless, we will continue with dignity and pride. It is very relaxing after a day's walk, when you can sit around and wait for darkness to arrive. It becomes very soothing listening to the quietness of the area. It has started to rain, and it looks like we are in for a storm, so I am going indoors to sort my backpack out for tomorrow. We haven't seen the little pest for some time now, maybe he has decided to go elsewhere.

DAY 22

This morning after eating breakfast around 8:30 a.m., we set off on what was the last leg of our incredible journey. It was a rough day today. Darryl and I had to climb more mountainous terrain. The backpacks are very heavy and awkward. It was hard bending all the time, so that your backpack wouldn't get caught in the bush or branches.

Almost every step, the packs would catch on something. It had been a nice warm day and each passing boat gave a toot on their horn as they passed by. Even Gordon Mackie on the Phoebe Ann honked his horn, as if to say "Go lake walkers Go".

The flowers are blooming now. We have now been gone 22 full days. Wow, that certainly seems like a long time. We had hiked thirteen and one quarter miles today, and we made it to Bastion Bay. We can now see the Trans-Canada Highway. We had met Mr. and Mrs. Brian Kraft today, who had converted a tugboat into a houseboat. It was so cool.

The mosquitoes are biting like mad again. Don and Betty Cowan are letting us use manual C.B's in case of an emergency, and are following us in their boat for the next day or so. They even caught a fish, and cleaned it for us for supper.

The scenery again is fantastic. All the boats are heading for home, as the people must get set for another day at work. You can tell that they had a good weekend, because its seven o'clock in the evening and they are just heading back. The water is very still right now, like a cobra, ready to strike its victim.
We are waiting for it to get dark, so we can see the headlights from the cars on the highway.

From where we are, the highway is cut along the mountain. It looks like a stitch job as it runs across. There is a creek running beside us, and the sound of its running water is so nice to hear. Yes, the Shuswap is a beautiful lake. It is very quiet and lonely at night.

We have truly learnt so much from this trip, not only about Shuswap Lake, but about the people and wilderness around it. The only words that I can say are the experience is its own teacher.

I have learnt so much about myself from this trip; that I know I will definitely be a better person when this mission is over. People have been great to us. It is so nice to see that people still care.

Darkness has once again set in on us, and we can now see the passing cars off in the distance. You could tell by their headlights flickering between the trees and mountains while they moved along.

Darryl is so happy to be that much closer to home. I think the trip is starting to get to Darryl now, but he knows that we don't have that much further to go.

It is very quiet out right now, and I have once again found peace of mind staring at the lights on the passing cars, and listening to the sounds of the creek beside us. What a beautiful feeling.

DAY 23

We have had a good rest from last night. Our shoulders are still very sore from carrying our packs, and our food supply is running low. Our only means of having a hot meal is to light a fire. Sometimes, this is impossible if it has rained out for a while. Before Max left, we had the Coleman stove to cook on.

We've had a very tough day today, and our progress was very slow. We managed to overcome cliff after cliff, like a giant stepping on a rock. We've gone too far for anything to happen now. We are camping at Totem Marina, and we are sore all over. We are drained of energy. I sure hope these hiking boots hold up because they are taking brutal punishment from the elements of this trip.

We really deserve to make this trip, and I mean it. We have been through everything, and for some reason- we have managed every item in our way. We should be home in three days or so, depending on the terrain ahead. We have done everything on this trek. If I had a chance to do it again, I wouldn't want to do it again without Darryl. He has been great, and I couldn't have gotten this far without him.

He also saved my life. We have stuck it out on this beautiful but sometimes treacherous trek around Shuswap Lake. I don't think there is a lake around as beautiful as this, and yet contain such beautiful wildlife, from all aspects.

It is like paradise, and I am happy to be part of it. People in the Shuswap area should be proud of this natural site, and work at keeping its upkeep. We have been blessed on this trip, and I thank God for that.

It is raining again now, and we just finished supper. We heard that the terrain up ahead is quite rough and we might be faced with the hardest part of our trip. I'm sure we will manage again, because we are the lake walkers.

We will finish the walk, because we are proud, and our pride is overwhelming. We are quite happy right now, and by the time we get to Sunnybrae, we will be that much happier.

There is not much that we can do right now because of the rain. It gets very chilly and damp when it rains out. I am going to enter the diary again.

The remainder of the night was rather boring as we were confined to the tent, because of the downpour.

DAY 24

We left the community of 'Totem' early this morning, and scored mile after mile. At the three mile mark on our pedometer around the area of Canoe Point Road, there was another huge cliff. Well, we sat in front of it, and eyed it up for about 10 minutes before climbing it. We started to climb, and increased each step two feet higher.

It took us a long time to climb up this huge cliff before we could come down. We were very high up on top of this mountain. I felt as though I should plant a flag or something to claim this mountain. Coming down one of these huge mountains was so much easier than going up. It always felt good being back on the ground.

After we succeeded this mountain; the shoreline was still rough. We met more people on our route and handed out more sighting forms. This walk takes a lot of energy out of you. Sometimes, after only the first hour of the day, you are tired. We kept going, as our pace seemed to be picking up, but that was only because we were so excited about being that much closer to the finish.

We arrived around the Sunnybrae neighborhood, and almost the whole community came out to greet us. What a feeling. Some people walked with us for a few hundred feet. We were walking on the beach with some of the area still rocky. Up ahead, we could see a swamp. It was around Sunnybrae Bible Camp. We waded our way through that obstacle, and then had two fences to cross. There was barbed wire on the top of these fences, and one of the wires tore into my skin just enough to make it bleed. I nursed my cut as I continued walking on.

Soakers after soakers, it was a wonder these hiking boots were still intact. They have been drenched 75% of the trip. Plunging on and on, we were determined to make it to Tappan before nightfall. Boy, were these packs heavy.

Shoreline mile after mile, we continued. Again, the bugs were after us, probably the same bugs from day one just following us around because they knew we were easy prey. Just as it was getting dark out, we arrived at Tappan.

I called Sally Scales from a lady named Yvonne, and told Sally that we would be resting up for a couple of days before completing the finish. We continued on to Tappan Co-op after crossing all the saturated shoreline in the Tappan area. We had been walking fifteen hours today, and we are starting to hallucinate once more.

The owner of Tappan Co-op, Ernie, said we could set up our tent beside his shed. We thanked Ernie, but when we saw it, the grass was very high, and the mosquitoes were like vampires.

We knew that we wouldn't be staying there, so I contacted Sally once again, and let her know that we wouldn't be staying at the Tappan Co-op, as planned. Being as busy as Sally always was, I couldn't reach her, so I contacted Jim Scales. Jim suggested we camp at Fraser's Point.

We thanked Ernie anyway, and continued on into the darkness toward Fraser's Point.

Darryl and I were completely exhausted, and were hallucinating all the way to Fraser's Point. We were walking like we were drunk, and we were slurring our words.

When we arrived at Fraser's Point, we said we were going to sleep under the stars because we were too exhausted to set up the tent but because of the fear of another storm, we did set up the tent. We were so tired, we passed our instantly. You couldn't wake us if you tried.

DAY 25

Last night, the winds were so strong that they blew the tent down four times. The winds were unreal. Throughout the night, the flapping of the tent would wake us up the odd time. As well as having the concern about our hiking boots lasting the rest of the trip, it is amazing that the tent has held up in the weather that we have been faced with.

We are going to rest for the whole day today. That's right, just sit around and take it easy. We are still beat from yesterday's walk, and last night's wind storms didn't help out much.

Tomorrow, we are going to do our final washing of our clothes this journey, and Friday we are going to finish the last 9 miles of our trip. I can't believe we are this close, only nine miles to the finish. Darryl has been a scout most of his life, and he finds it hard to believe that he has been part of such a physical, mental, and an emotional venture.

It has been 25 days, and that's a long time in the bush for anyone. The remainder of the day, we just dozed on and off, and tried to get some strength back. Yesterday's walk really hurt us. We were hallucinating so bad that when you looked at the ground; it looked like worms moving around, when in fact, there was nothing there. We were on the brink of total exhaustion.

DAY 26

Here we are, yet another day at Fraser's Point. We are pretty well out of supplies, including food. We may be over the 400-mile mark by the time we are done. We aren't sure yet, we will have to see at the finish. We are relaxing now, and preparing for the finish.

The backpacks have been put through the mill. Some of the pain that we have been feeling has gone. It could be that we are no longer thinking of pain, only the finish line. We met some people today who offered us to join them in their home to watch some slides, seeing it was our last night before completing this trip.

Our washing was done, and it was now drying. We are going to have everything packed before going to visit with these people. We expect to be visiting late, and want to be ready right away in the morning. Just after what was to be our final supper outdoors, we went to watch slides with the people we had met. The company was nice, and it made us feel good.

Coincidentally, the slides that we were watching were about another lake that had hardly any shoreline. The people said "how would you like to walk around this?" I said "no thanks", and laughed.

We watched the slides until 11:00p.m. After several coffees, we decided to turn in for the night, and get prepared mentally for tomorrow. We thanked our gracious guests before leaving.

When we went back to our tent, both Darryl and I talked about tomorrow for a while. We really have gone a long way. Our bodies have become very solid and stronger.

Darryl looked like he lost about 30 pounds, and me, I tightened my belt a couple of notches. We were starting to think about what it will be like to finally finish what we had started.

The remainder of the night was a good quiet one. I entered my diary again, and even read a little of it before falling asleep.

DAY 27

It was now time to head out from Frasers Point. We were all rested up and ready for the last 9 miles of THE FIRST WALK AROUND SHUSWAP LAKE. We were so excited and happy that we started singing as we hiked through marsh and soggy areas.

It was hot out this final day, and we began to sweat again. A train just passed by us going westbound, and he honked his big air horn at us. I was happy. Darryl had tears in his eyes. Tears of joy, that is. Other than marshy areas, the final nine miles were pretty well straight forward.

As we approached Salmon Arm, our eyes stared right in front of us to the finish. Work in the Salmon Arm area had carried on as usual today. Noca Dairy and Newness Machine were operating at full capacity. Did people remember about us, or had they forgotten about us? We thought.

We were to meet Sally and the girls from Shoppers Guide, one mile from the finish, and they were to walk with us the last remaining steps of our month long journey.

Sure enough, there they were, but one mile seemed too far for them, so they met us about a quarter of a mile from the Salmon Arm Marina, and walked as they promised, to the end.

I couldn't believe it, the first walk around Shuswap Lake had now been completed. It was a joyous occasion for the area, as well as Darryl and I. For the people that showed up for the return, I'm sure that this walk will always remain in their minds.

The local newspapers were there, as we handed over an envelope containing the final mileage recorded in our 27-day adventure.

The official mileage around the four arms of Shuswap Lake was 386.5 miles. This was covered in a 27 day period, between May 19th, 1979, and June 15th, 1979.

Handshakes and pictures were taken, than it was a chauffeured ride through downtown Salmon Arm. We were like heroes being paraded around in the back of Dale Lines 1964 Pontiac convertible.

Several times, we stopped to shake hands with several of the towns' people. I was sure proud of both Darryl and myself. Everyone in town was quite happy at our return.

The celebration didn't end at the parade through town, but continued to the 7th Rib Steakhouse for supper. We had a choice of anything that we wanted. I ordered the largest order that they had, and Darryl ordered the same.

We ate to our hearts delight, and celebrated in jubilation. A nice group of people accompanied our table and listened to stories of our adventure. The night slowly started to drift away, and it was time to lay back, gain some peace of mind, and just be content.

Dan and Darrell thanked Don Ewart, partner in the Seventh Rib restaurant, for a delicious steak dinner, compliments of the restaurant, and told him Shuswap Lake has a shoreline 386½ miles in length.

Many sighted the Lake Walkers

By Vicky Johnson

The Shuswap Walkers completed their trek around Shuswap Lake on Friday, June 15.

Darrell Kelly and Dan Goodale handed out forms to people they met as they walked, and they asked each person to fill out these forms and send them to the Chamber of Commerce in Salmon Arm. Forty-two letters have been received from viewers of the Shuswap Walkers, and a few more may still be on the way.

A large map of the lake is on display at the Chamber of Commerce visitors' information office, and the map is marked with slips of paper showing the times and places where the boys were sighted. Very few letters were sent from Seymour Arm and Anstey Arm, where fewer people live.

The Lake Walkers also left behind bottles containing notes, and so far only one has been reported found. Ric Porteous of Salmon Arm found a bottle containing a note reading "Narrows, May 22." The bottle was found on a line between 2-mile logging camp and Beach Bay on Seymour Arm.

Lakewalkers complete trek

"We were not out to get a tan," was the comment by Dan Goodall, one of the Lake Walkers, when he strolled into the News to report on the 27 day trek of recording the exact miles of the Shuswap Lake foreshore.

On May 19th, the historic trek began at Salmon Arm when two walkers and one canoist were determined to record the exact miles of Shuswap Lake. Dan Goodall and Darrell Kelly clocked the mileage of the four Arms of the Shuswap at 386½ miles, the hard way.

Climbing and clutching on to the cliffs, one which had a 260 ft. verticle drop, lead to "great emotional pressures, but we had too much pride to turn back," said Darrell Kelly. Struggling along the west side of the Lake they walked from 9 a.m. to one o'clock in the morning before they could find a camp-site. The area was in the "big burn of 1967", where windfalls, debris and cliffs made it almost impossible to break through. On a scale of 1 - 10, the trek was measured as "9" in toughness was the opinion of the two men who aspire to have the feat recorded in the Guiness Book of Records. "We feel that no one else will succeed in completing the trip," said Kelly. Apparently the canoeist, Max Wilde, concurred with this statement, as he abandoned the project near Scotch Creek. He simply beached the canoe and silently stole away. It is believed he headed back to Ontario. This necessitated Goodall and Kelly to back-pack limited supplies for the balance of the trip to the destination point of Salmon Arm.

The accuracy of the measurement for the mileage of the Shuswap was questioned by the News. The walkers tallied the four Arms of the Lake at 386½, whereas it has always been claimed to be "over 1000 miles of lakeshore". (The walkers did not measure Mara Lake or the Little Shuswap.

Confusion on the definition of Shuswap Lake and the Shuswap Lake System has led to some people questioning the mileage recorded by the walkers.

In a Dominion Survey undertaken in 1880-1900's, lead by John Smith the Lake System was surveyed from Shuswap River to Enderby, Mara Lake, Anstey Arm, Seymour Arm, Salmon Arm, Big Shuswap, Little Shuswap, Little River, South Thompson to Kamloops, North Thompson to Barriere and all of the Kamloops Lake from Savona east.

This was **not** the route the Lake Walkers took. They measured **all four arms** of the Shuswap Lake using Taylor Pedometers. Both walkers carried the pedometers which were only ¼ of a mile out in difference. The Walkers may measure Mara Lake and the Little Shuswap to include the miles in the tally.

In a brief interview with the manager of the Salmon Arm Chamber of Commerce, Mrs. Routledge, agreed that the definition of "1000 miles of foreshore" could be misleading, and paramount to discussing "apples and oranges" - the Shuswap Lake and the Shuswap Lake System had not been clearly defined to the Walkers. "perhaps we should define Shuswap Lake to end any further confusion."

Routledge said he thought the Lake Walkers did a credible job, although we were a bit disappointed in the mileage recorded. The Chamber intend to have the two adventurers address the Chamber and present their slides of the trip at a future meeting.

The two walkers registered some discontent with the news reports of the walk. Contrary to other papers it was reported that several organizations had visited them on the walk. Goodall said the only person to visit them "on site" was the reporter of the Eagle Valley news. They also stated it was reported their 22's were confiscated. "Not so", say the walkers, "We turned them over voluntarily at Scotch Creek". Another rumor was that they had shot a bear. "Not so" say the walkers, "we shot in the water at Broken Point, near Anstey Arm, when the bears took three packs of supplies, one which included my wallet," said Goodall. In explanation of shooting into the water, "we felt the loud echo ricocheting from the mountains would frighten them off."

Another problem which troubled the walkers was the marking of the foreshore with orange flourescent paint, which was abandoned early in the trip, Goodall said he had checked with the R.C.M.P. and only 3 or 4 complaints were registered, **not** a barrage as reported in the papers, said Goodall. The Walkers expressed regret at over-enthusiasm of marking the trail.

386½ miles on Shuswap say walkers

Lakeshore Walkers, Dan Goodale and Darrell Kelly reported to the News the miles of the four arms of the Shuswap Lake is 386 and one half mile. Only area not walked was the Mara Lake and Little Shuswap.

They started the walk May 19th and completed the walk on Friday, June 15th.

More story next week on the trials and tribulations of walking the lakeshore.

To know that the entire shoreline around Shuswap Lake was circumnavigated on foot; is an achievement in itself.

This journey will always play a major role in my life. I am thankful that the challenge was offered and accepted.

I will always honor this achievement. It doesn't matter the size of Shuswap Lake. All that matters is that all people concerned about this area, take care and respect it.

Shuswap Lake is by far the most beautiful lake that I have ever witnessed. Its beauty and serenity speaks for itself.

As for the people living around the lake, I have never met such nice and polite people in all of my life.

Without their help on this incredible journey, I doubt if we would have been able to finish.

This is definitely God's country, and I pray that modernization respects this area.

A Personal Note

I hope that you have enjoyed reading 27 Days Around Shuswap Lake.

This is a true story that took place from May 19th to June 15th, 1979.

The story was rewritten from a personal diary that I kept, during our 27-day adventure, where we utilized the 'buddy-system' to fulfill this accomplishment.

Our journey was recorded to be three hundred and eighty-six, and one half miles of rugged shoreline circumnavigated on foot.

At times, without God's help, we would not have succeeded in completing this trek.

I hope that this story teaches you that if you are determined enough to accomplish something, and really believe in what you are doing, then you will succeed.

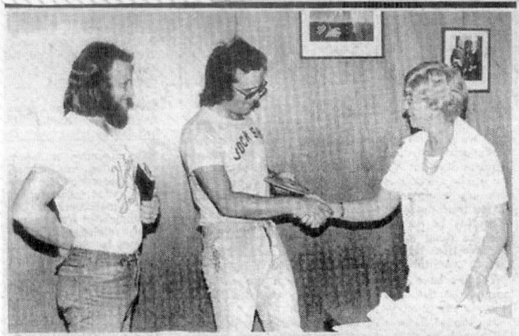

Mayor Margaret Lund presented engraved plaques to the Shuswap Walkers, Dan Goodale, left, and Darrell Kelly at council June 25th. Each plaque reads: In recognition of his achievement of walking the entire shoreline.

The two men reported on their trip, and said they were going to have the diary of their trip printed, and one copy will be presented to the Salmon Arm library.

Sally Scales photo

LAKE WALKERS RETURN. Darrel Kelly, left, and Dan Goodall climb aboard a Dale Lines chauffeured convertible for a ride through town at the conclusion of their 386½-mile lake hike Friday. Riding with them is Tony Wawrzyniak who offered the walkers a good deal of advice and experience, and kept in contact with them during their long journey.

Shoreline report: 386½ miles

Twenty seven days and 386½ miles later Dan Goodale and Darrell Kelly are back from what many think is the first-ever walk around the entire shoreline of Shuswap Lake. In the process they made liars of those who estimated the distance at closer to 1800 miles and wished them on their way with the words: "See you in December."

For Goodale and Kelly the entire trip was a lesson in determination, a trip which forced them to accept at different times natural obstacles, human failings and their own fears.

At one point half-way through the walk near Scotch Creek the Lakewalkers found their provisions canoe abandoned on the beach — the canoeist gone without any warning, apparently returned to Ontario after deciding the trip around the lake was just too much for him.

For the rest of the walk Goodale and Kelly were forced to carry all provisions on their backs. At night after a 10-hour day walking over the wild terrain, they began to boil fiddlehead ferns to supplement their diet.

At times the pair found themselves wading through creeks with water up to their chests and then on the same day clinging to the face of a cliff with a 260-foot verticle drop to the water and rocks below.

Once, what looked like a solid hand-hold turned out to be a geological fault and a 700 pound boulder hurtled past them into the lake. The experience left them, they said; "shaken."

A fear the two had from the beginning — an attack from hungry bears, came true one evening and three bags of provisions were lost to the animals before they could be driven off by shots from a .22 rifle.

Goodale's and Kelly's difficulties were not limited solely to natural hardships but included the human variety as well.

RCMP confiscated their .22 rifles after shots were fired to scare off the bears and some days earlier the Lake Walkers were forced to give up the idea of marking their trail with orange fluorescent paint when a barrage of complaints brought the Mounties down on them again.

Continued on page 2

Lake walkers

Continued from page 1

Most of the painting was done below high water mark and will eventually be washed away, they claim, but admit; "we got a little carried away with it."

Perhaps the strangest experience the two had on the entire trip was a meeting with a hermit who, "would be talking just like us," and then start singing Indian songs, talked of the devil and the spirit of Black Cloud. In the back of his makeshift house there were bones to ward off evil spirits.

In the end both Goodale and Kelly agree that the trip was worth the experience but there are some regrets.

When they got back to Salmon Arm after 26 days there were no brass bands and no large welcome. They felt as if, "nobody came to see us off and nobody came to welcome us home."

Still the two Lake Walkers are proud of their accomplishment and will attempt to have it entered in the Guiness Book of Records under human achievements.

Verification

CHBC
OKANAGAN TELEVISION

OKANAGAN VALLEY TELEVISION COMPANY LIMITED
TELEX 048-5119   PHONE (604) 762-4535

342 LEON AVENUE, KELOWNA, B.C.
CANADA V1Y 6J2

Dan Goodale,

Congratulations on completing your trek around the Shuswap.

I hope future trips by you can be even more successful and enjoyable.

Mike Robert

To whom it may concern—

This is to advise that the persons, known as Dave Goodall and Darryl Kelly, did, according to reliable sources, circumnavigate four arms of the Shuswap lake, section we float.

They began the undertaking on May 19th 1979, with the object of measuring the total distance of the shoreline. It was ended on June 13th 1979, twenty-nine days and three hundred and eighty-six miles later.

This, to the best of my knowledge, is the first time that such an undertaking has been attempted.

[signature]
Manager.

July 9, 1979

TO WHOM IT MAY CONCERN

This is to confirm that, to the best of our knowledge,
the persons known as DAN GOODALE and DARRYL KELLY did,
in fact, circumnavigate the shoreline of the four arms
of Shuswap Lake on foot, having done so in a period of
29 days commencing May 19, 1979 and ending June 15, 1979.

This confirmation is based on the receipt of 43 written
reported sightings of the two "walkers" and further
supported by several other verbal reports of people
encountering the "walkers" in their travels.

Sincerely,

SALMON ARM AND DISTRICT
CHAMBER OF COMMERCE

Neville A. Hutton
President

NAH/tb

Province of British Columbia
OFFICE OF THE DEPUTY PREMIER

July 16, 1979

Mr. Darrell Kelly,
General Delivery,
Salmon Arm, British Columbia,
V0E 2T0

Dear Darrell,

In recognition of your 27 day journey covering 386½ miles of Shuswap Lake in this Year of the Child and the Family in British Columbia, I am pleased to send you a medallion commemorating your generous and brave endeavour.

Sincerely,

Grace M. McCarthy,
Deputy Premier

Encl.

Years Later

Years later, after the walk around Shuswap Lake had been completed, here are some interesting things to note:

- When the pictures of the Hermit were developed, only the pictures of his makeshift cabin turned out. Even though we know that we took several pictures of him, no picture of the hermit ever turned out. It was as though, he was a spirit.

- 43 people out of all the people that we met walking around the lake, sent in the sighting forms to the Salmon Arm Chamber of Commerce. The Chamber erected a huge map of Shuswap Lake, encased in glass with flags pinned to the areas around the lake where the 43 people had seen and talked to us. This map is on display at the Salmon Arm Museum.

- Of the several notes in the bottles that were dropped off at several points around the lake, one was found by Rick Porteous 10 years after it was dropped off.

- A slide essay for the town was made with 253 slides of the walk around the lake. This slide essay was narrated by Darryl and I.

- The attempt to be acknowledged in the Guinness Book of World Records was not approved. However, since then, some conditions and rules have changed, and a re-submission of the information has been sent for review.

- We received an Olympic Metal from the Honorable Grace McCarthy, for our achievement.

- We received an engraved Plaque, from Mayor Margaret Lund of Salmon Arm.

- People who have read 27 Days Around Shuswap Lake are convinced the story has brought them warmth from within.

- No one has attempted to walk around Shuswap Lake since and our walk around Shuswap Lake is now Historic!.

About The Author

Dan Goodale was born in Port Moody, British Columbia.
He now lives in Ontario, and has never lost his love for the
beauty of British Columbia. His twenty-seven day adventure
around Shuswap Lake has always remained a fond memory, thus
compelling him to finally tell his story.

still hiking

Manufactured by Amazon.ca
Acheson, AB

10289284R00083